My Mary

MY MARY

PATSY MACDONALD

MY MARY
Copyright © 2012, Patsy MacDonald

All Rights Reserved. No part of this publication may be reproduced, stored in a retrieval system or transmitted in any form or by any means—electronic, mechanical, photocopy, recording or any other— except for brief quotations in printed reviews, without the prior permission of the author.

New Revised Standard Version Bible: Catholic Edition, copyright 1989, 1993, Division of Christian Education of the National Council of the Churches of Christ in the United States of America. Used by permission. All rights reserved.

ISBN: 978-1-4600-0008-3
LSI Edition: 978-1-4600-0009-0
E-book ISBN: 978-1-4600-0010-6
(E-book available from the Kindle Store, KOBO and the iBookstore)

Cataloguing data available from Library and Archives Canada

To order additional copies, visit:
www.essencebookstore.com

For more information, please contact:
Patsy MacDonald
mymary@bellaliant.net

Published by Angels Publishing

Printed in Belleville, Ontario Canada by Essence Publishing.

Dedication

I would like to dedicate this book to all the laity, who put so much effort and love into serving God throughout our churches.

May you all be blessed for all your dedication to serving others.

Acknowledgments

A special thank you to Adam's parents, David and DeeDee O'Neil, who so willingly allowed me to share some of their son's journey.

To my husband, Peter, my rock, who has given me so much love, support, and encouragement to share my own spiritual journey.

To my children, Melissa and Amanda, who helped me to keep focused when I became discouraged.

To all my family, friends, and people who God put in my path who supported me in any way with the writing of this book, which allowed me to share my own moments of grace that I have been given the privilege of experiencing.

Contents

Introduction 11
Adam's Diagnosis (November 2002) 17
Adam's Passing (November 17, 2005) 23
Telling Adam's Mom (December 16, 2005) 31
Planning of the Rosary Garden (January 2006) 35
First Anniversary of Adam's Death (November 17, 2006)..........39
In the Garden with Jesus (November 25, 2006) 43
Death Is a Natural Process 47
    Dad
    Nan
    Mom
    Camille
Rainbows 73
Building the Rosary Garden (June 23, 2007) 81
What Is Your Calling? 87
Sketch of Jesus (November 2007) 93
Feast Day of the Lady of the Rosary 97
Adoration (May 20, 2008) 103
Palliative Care Volunteer 109
The Messenger (July 17, 2008) 115
Healing (July 27, 2008) 123

Bereavement Work 129
Divine Mercy (April 18, 2009) 135
Foot of the Cross (May 2009) 141
Walk with Jesus on the Beach (June 2009) 147
Lenten Mission (March 2010) 153
Gifts of Tongues (April 16, 2010) 155
Vision of the Blessed Mother (January 11, 2011) 159
Our Lady of the Pond (May 8, 2011) 165
Beautiful Teaching Moment (May 14, 2011) 171
Protection from our Blessed Mother (May 24, 2011) 175
A Numinous Moment (June 7, 2011) 181
Life Lessons (September 2011) 185
Come, See, Go, Tell 189
Will You Carry My Son in Your Heart? 193
References 197

Introduction

People cross our paths every day.

It is impossible to know what kind of impact these people, or our meetings with them, will have on our lives. As I look back over the course of my life, I realize none of these acquaintances are merely coincidences. They come into our lives to help us grow. Sometimes their time with us is brief, but when we consider the vastness of life, time can be considered to be almost irrelevant. What matters is what we give and receive from each other. The experience of crossing paths.

His name was Adam. To me, Adam was just an ordinary kid I'd seen around our neighbourhood. My husband, Peter, had known Adam's mom, DeeDee, when they were growing up. It was many years later I got to know DeeDee, and probably a year before Adam's passing my friendship with her began to blossom.

And yet somehow upon this ordinary boy's death, everything about my life changed. I will always be thankful that because of him, because of our brief crossing of paths, I have a closer relationship with our Blessed Mother.

I was brought up Catholic, and Sunday Mass was a big part of my growing up years. I attended Mass with my dad. My mom, unfortunately, couldn't join us because she suffered with claustrophobia. She made up for it, though. I remember many nights after the lights had switched off, settling under the covers and hearing her call, "Did you say your prayers?"

My Mary

My dad died when I was thirteen, and my life was filled with turmoil after that. I felt like a part of my heart went with him when he left. The only thing that helped me get through that time was a sense that Jesus was watching over me. It seemed only while I was attending Mass did I feel some type of normalcy in my life.

Even as a young girl I felt a close bond to Jesus, and for many years I sensed Him watching over me. My older sister gave me a book called *Letters to God* shortly after Dad died. Seeing the book was filled with letters written by teenagers helped me to understand, even at an early age, that I could turn to Him when I needed someone to listen to me, to share my hurt over the loss of my dad, to express how hard it was to adjust to this new life. I knew in my heart that at least He would listen.

A few years after Adam died, I began looking back over all the grace-filled moments I'd been given the privilege of experiencing. This story was triggered on the night of Adam's death, but actually began a couple of years before, at an angel workshop I attended at our local library with a friend.

For many years I'd had a fascination with angels. At one time I had seriously considered opening my own angel shop. In the end, I realized I wasn't willing to take on the responsibility of owning my own business. What I really wanted was to be around people whose spirituality was important to them.

I believe the angels began their work on the night of the workshop. Adam's mom, DeeDee, was there, and though we had both arrived at the workshop with separate friends, we chatted before it began. I asked DeeDee how her two boys, Adam, and his younger brother, Cameron, were doing. When she told me Adam was looking for part-time work while attending university, I mentioned that the office where my husband was employed often hired young men to merchandise the company's stock.

Introduction

"I'll mention that to Adam," she said, smiling. "Maybe he can get in touch with Peter to find out more about it."

I believe the connection that was supposed to be made occurred that evening. That was the beginning of my spiritual journey, a journey that would take me through a whirlwind of emotions: love, hurt, disappointment, and healing. When I look back over everywhere I've been, the most important thing on which I try to focus is love. At the end of the day, and especially at the end of our lives, what's most important is how we loved, even though it might sometimes have been easier not to.

Adam began working at the same company as my husband a short time later. He was still employed there at the time of his death on November 17, 2005.

Adam with his Mom and Dad at his High School Graduation

My Mary

I am writing this book six years later. Ever since the night of Adam's death, I have had spiritual experiences, though it took me many years to realize that these were moments of grace that I had been given the privilege of having. A friend once suggested that I write down all these experiences as I was having them. She thought maybe someday I would need to go back to these times in my life, and it might be helpful to have dates recorded. I believe she knew in her heart that one day I would be sharing my experiences with others. It seems God always puts the right people in your path when He has plans for you.

A Time for Everything

For everything there is a season,
and a time for every matter under heaven:
a time to be born, and a time to die;
a time to plant, and a time to pluck up what is planted;
a time to kill, and a time to heal;
a time to break down, and a time to build up;
a time to weep, and a time to laugh;
a time to mourn, and a time to dance;
a time to throw away stones, and a time to gather stones together;
a time to embrace, and a time to refrain from embracing;
a time to seek, and a time to lose;
a time to keep, and a time to throw away;
a time to tear, and a time to sew;
a time to keep silence, and a time to speak;
a time to love, and a time to hate;
a time for war, and a time for peace
(Ecclesiastes 3:1-8).

Introduction

I've kept the idea of writing a book in the back of my mind for a while. So why do I now feel the need to share my moments of grace? I'm the type of person who relies strongly on intuition, using it to make life decisions. I believe intuition is God whispering to us. As the Bible verse goes, there is a time for everything. I sensed this was the right time for me to share my spiritual journey, and about a month before I started writing, I had another spiritual experience. That was a clear sign to me that the timing was right.

Later in the book I'll share this experience as well as other grace-filled moments. My hope is that you will realize each one of us is capable of receiving their own moments of grace. God loves all of us. He wants to share gifts with us so that we may use them to bring others close to Him.

Life gets so hectic that most of us don't slow down and listen to His whispers. We don't take time from our busy day to spend with Him in prayer. My wish for you is that you give yourself the opportunity of experiencing your own moments of grace. These moments are waiting for each and every one of us.

Adam's Diagnosis

(November 2002)

In August 2002, Adam O'Neil began to experience bouts of nausea. He would be in the shower, getting ready for work, and suddenly start to get sick. He started calling in to work from time to time, too sick to do his shift. In November, Adam was diagnosed with a rare form of cancer. The specialists told his family there was only one other person in Canada who had been diagnosed with the same kind.

This is the type of news no family wants to hear. There is something about children being diagnosed with such an illness that just doesn't seem normal. I remember gazing down at the newborn face of my first child, Melissa, holding her in my arms and whispering, "I will love and protect you always." But we come to realize we cannot protect them from everything.

I remember hearing at a talk I attended years earlier that our children come through us, but are not from us. They are God's children. It made me realize that no matter what, they will have to go through their own journey. We hope our children will know that on this journey, they will never be alone. By His grace and love for them, He will always be right beside them, through all of their life struggles.

The next three years were a roller coaster of emotions for Adam's immediate family, his relatives, and the friends of his family. What began in September as a promising future for a young man beginning university became one of uncertainty for the family.

With all the emotional turmoil going on in his family, Adam himself exuded a surprising strength and calmness you couldn't help but notice. His main concerns never seemed to be for himself. He wanted to be sure any news they had to relay to Grandma O'Neil or to Adam's friends was told without upsetting them too much.

Adam (r) with Cameron and Grandma O'Neil

I believe Adam was an old soul. He knew the adults in his life would eventually accept what he was going through, but he understood it would be harder on his elderly grandmother and on the young people. The elderly, of course, are more fragile; most young people simply believe they are immortal.

What a blessing this family was for the rest of us. Even though they were in so much pain, they taught us about how important it is to give and receive love and support. What really stood out to those of us looking in from the outside, was how close a bond both David and DeeDee had with their extended families.

It was beautiful to witness how Adam and Cameron had grown up, surrounded by so much love from their Grandma O'Neil, their aunts, uncles, and cousins. It reminded us all of how we should each live our own lives. The blessing for this family was that although they had been given such a heavy cross to bear, they would not be carrying it alone.

It was not a surprise to the rest of us when we saw, on the day of Adam's funeral, how many of the quotes written about him allowed relative strangers to understand what a special young man he truly was.

"We will remember the grace, dignity, and serenity he displayed every day of this life."

"Those of us who were privileged to know and love Adam knew his illness never took hope from him. It never destroyed his spirit."

"Adam's passion for life, his ability to 'wring the juice' out of every day, was inspiring."

We learned that even when Adam was much younger, he seemed to understand that God was an important part of his life.

DeeDee had often asked him what he was doing, and he would say, "I'm talking to God, Mom."

One day when Adam was little, he was in the bathroom and he was taking a long time. DeeDee became concerned and went to check on him. She found him sitting on the toilet, pulling the little squares of toilet paper apart, stacking them one on top of the other.

"Adam, what are you doing?" DeeDee asked.

"I'm playing a game with God," he replied.

My Mary

Adam with Most Reverend Terrence Prendergast at his Confirmation

At the funeral, the family shared a story about the time Adam came to DeeDee with a list of what he wanted for Christmas. DeeDee told him his list was too long and he could only ask Santa for two presents. If he was a really good boy, she told him, maybe his parents would also give him a couple.

She took the opportunity to explain that lots of children needed presents, so Santa couldn't bring him everything he wanted. She stressed how important it was for him to share with others. Adam left the room, not pleased with this news, and DeeDee assumed that was the end of the discussion. Like any other parent, she was pleased to have been able to teach him this important lesson.

Being a mother myself, I understand that often we question our parenting skills. Did we say or do the correct thing when it came to teaching our children? In DeeDee's heart she knew she had done a good job with the explanation, and she hoped her son would now better understand the importance of sharing with others.

Adam's Diagnosis

A short while later, Adam came back to DeeDee. "Mom," he said, "I was just speaking to God. He told me that He's Santa's boss, so I can have whatever I want."

Adam (l) with Cameron and Santa Daddy

My Mary

Out of the mouths of babes. How many times do our children say similar things to us and we just pass them off as being cute? We don't always see that there may be more meaningful things going on that we don't understand at the time.

Looking back on all that we came to learn about Adam, it's no surprise that the baby boy his mom and dad had brought home from the hospital years before would eventually bring people closer to our Blessed Mother. This little boy was special. The people who loved him the most stood back and watched as he became a young man, dealing with a terminal illness with grace, dignity, and serenity.

Adam's Passing
(November 17, 2005)

Shortly before Adam died, his parents held an auction for him in their hometown, hoping to raise enough money to send him to New York. They had been told there was a clinic there that had previously helped someone suffering with the same type of cancer Adam had. They were optimistic that maybe they could get help for their son there, because nothing that had been done up to this point was helping.

The people from the company where both my husband and Adam had worked decided they would also raise money to help out with this expense. That evening, when Peter came home from work, he asked me where I had put a jar he'd been planning to take to work the next day. He said the employees wanted to put money in it, to add to the auction amount.

I was on my way out the door to go to a meeting at our parish, but I stopped to get the jar for Peter, then he and I had a short chat about Adam, empathizing about how difficult this must be on the family. At least, we agreed, they had a supportive community. Everyone who knew the O'Neils wanted to help in any way they could. Everyone wanted them to know they were not alone in this fight.

Before I share with you what happened to me on the way to the meeting, and the reaction that I had, I think it's important for you to know some of my career background. I had spent three and

My Mary

a half years working as a ward clerk in the Pediatric Intensive Care Unit before I changed jobs, moving to a women's clinic in the same hospital. I had made this change only a month before Adam died. My background, before I went to work in the hospital, was in banking and insurance, other than a period when I worked six months in a medical clinic.

I don't believe it is common for an individual to go from a career of banking and insurance to working in an intensive care unit in a hospital. Over lunch one day I was speaking with one of the nurses, and she seemed very surprised when I told her my work background. But the change of pace didn't bother me. I seemed able to adapt well to the high-energy, often stressful place to work. But the position could also be very emotional. It is so important to have compassion for others in this type of setting. People need to be able to count on you for strength when they feel they have none left.

Before I started in the Pediatric Intensive Care Unit, I had a strong urge to change jobs. I had known a nurse who worked in the unit, and when a temporary job came up, she suggested I apply for it. It certainly wasn't the type of atmosphere in which I had been planning to spend the rest of my career. When I was offered the job, I had to pray hard about it, because I wasn't sure if this was where I should be working.

I feared I lacked the experience that would allow me to work effectively in an intensive care unit, but my intuition kept telling me otherwise. Paying attention to those whispers won over my fear, and before I knew it I was caught up in the hustle and bustle of an active PICU unit.

Today I am eternally glad I listened to my intuition. Working there taught me so much about death and how we cannot take anything in life for granted. Things can happen very quickly in our lives. One minute things are great, but without any warning, our lives can be changed forever.

Adam's Passing

The type of unit in which I worked was an open one. Most of the beds were separated by curtains. When a child was dying, you were in the same room with both them and their family. There were also three separate rooms in the unit, but the child was not always in those rooms when they died.

Although a curtain was pulled for privacy, you knew when a child was dying. It was so painful to see the devastation in the families' faces. I am a mother of two girls, and it tore my heart out to see the moms, some of whom hadn't had a lot of time to prepare, trying to let go of their children. It also gave me the opportunity to see how differently we all react when faced with death.

I am convinced that this was exactly where God wanted me to be. He needed me to understand about death and dying. By my learning and experiencing these things, I would be better able to do what He asked when He saw I was ready to comfort His people.

I believe that is why I had the reaction I did, when I was driving to my parish the night Adam died. On my way there, I had to drive by the street where the O'Neils lived.

That is where I had a vision. Jesus appeared before me, along with Adam, who stood on Jesus's left side. They were both wearing white gowns. I knew Adam had died in that moment.

Before Jesus could speak to me, I actually yelled at Him. "I can't believe what you do to mothers!"

I was so upset. In my heart, all I could understand was that He had taken Adam from his mom. But Jesus gazed into my eyes. Very calmly, He said, "I understand because of my own mother."

Calmness spread through my body as He said this to me, and I knew Jesus really did understand. Not only did His mom have to lose her Son, but she had to stand by and watch as He was being tortured.

For those whose hearts are hurting from losing their child, you need to know that the Blessed Mother does understand your pain. If you turn to her in these times, she can help bring comfort to your heart.

Jesus gave me three messages about Adam:

"He has very important work to do."

"She will be so proud of him." (He didn't say DeeDee's name.)

"He will be famous."

The vision ended, and I kept driving to my meeting.

Although Adam hadn't spoken, I could sense he was listening intently. I knew it was important to him that I listen to what Jesus had to say. I understood Adam was on his way with Jesus to do the important work of which Jesus spoke, and I had the feeling that Adam was very comfortable being with Jesus. In my heart I believed it was important to both him and Jesus that the messages were being relayed to someone who would eventually share them.

I can still see this vision in my mind as if it just happened. I realize how hard it might be to understand what I'm saying if you have never had this type of experience. How, you might ask, could I possibly be driving a car at the same time as I saw and had a conversation with Jesus? The truth is, I don't understand it myself. But what I've come to understand over time is that when Jesus gives us such graces, we don't need to put our energy into understanding why or how. It's more important for us to use what we experience so we can help people understand that He's really not that far from us. How comforting it is for us to know that when our lives are in turmoil and we hurt, Jesus understands. After all, He walked the earth as we do now. Like us, He had to go through the emotional turmoil that living brings.

I arrived at my meeting as if nothing had just taken place. It was almost as if it hadn't happened. Like my brain didn't register it.

Adam's Passing

The one thing that stood out in my mind about that night at the meeting was hearing sirens wailing from an ambulance outside. I remember hoping that whoever the ambulance was going for was okay. I'm not sure if this was the ambulance that came for Adam, but because of the timing, it is a possibility.

I remember coming home from the meeting and telling my husband that I had Adam on my mind all night, though I didn't go into detail about what I had experienced. My brain still wasn't accepting that this was possible. How could I have had a conversation with Jesus? I didn't give it much more thought as I went to bed for the night.

The next morning while I was at work, the phone rang. It was my husband, Peter.

"I have some bad news," he said. He told me DeeDee's neighbour, Maria, had called to tell him that Adam had passed away the night before. Adam had been playing football with his friends and died on the field because of a blood clot caused by the cancer treatments. The last thing Adam had said to his mom before going out that evening was, "I love you."

I was in shock. This made no sense. People didn't usually drop dead from cancer. It was usually a longer, more gradual illness. I was so upset I could barely think. Then I remembered the night before.

"Peter," I said, "I saw Adam with Jesus last night, as I was on my way to the meeting. What time did he die?"

"I think it was around nine o'clock," he replied.

I was confused. How could I have seen Adam on my way to the meeting, which was shortly after seven, if he hadn't died until nine o'clock? I kept pondering this all day, asking myself how I could have possibly seen someone a few hours before they died.

It was only after I calmed down and really started to think about all that had taken place that another thought came to me.

My Mary

I had been given an opportunity to see and speak to Jesus, and what had I done? I had yelled at Him for hurting mothers. I couldn't believe I'd done that, but as I thought about it, I had to smile. I knew Jesus would understand. He knew I had always tried to protect people from getting hurt. Why would I be any different when I met Him?

When I came home from work that day, I still felt dazed. I needed to talk to someone so I could make sense of what I had experienced; however, this was not the type of conversation I could have with just anyone. My friend Roseann came to mind. She and I had shared many spiritual discussions in the past, and I knew she would understand better than anyone. She wouldn't judge or make fun of me.

People have a sense of who they can share things with and who they can't. That's rather sad, when you think about it. If people could openly share how they really felt about their spirituality, others could learn from them. It could help them find the peace in their hearts that a lot of people are seeking, the peace that comes from having a close relationship to Jesus. But some people don't understand, and some are uncomfortable with the idea.

I feel very blessed that I have someone with whom I could share my experience. I believe one of the reasons God put her in my life was that when I had this spiritual experience, I would have someone to whom I could turn. He knew I could go to her for advice, and her own spirituality could help calm me.

When I called Roseann, I could barely wait for her to answer the phone. When she did, I was so relieved. Finally I could share something I was having a hard time understanding. She listened intently and soothed my fears. Even though she didn't understand why this had happened to me, she strongly believed it was God's plan. She said sometimes we don't understand the way God works in our lives, but we have to trust in Him.

Adam's Passing

Roseann didn't know Adam's family, but she was saddened to hear a young man had died. She told me that no matter how hard it would be for me, I had a responsibility to tell his mother what had happened: that I had seen her son with Jesus the night he died. She felt it was important for DeeDee to know the messages Jesus had given me about both her and her son.

I felt much more peaceful after I spoke to Roseann. I thought about her advice and realized this would be an opportunity for me to learn. I had to trust that God knew why this should happen.

However, the next day, while I was driving my sixteen-year-old daughter, Amanda, to work, I told her about the experience I'd had the night before. She wasn't sure it was such a great idea for me to tell people about this. I believe she was concerned about people getting hurt.

I explained to her that since I was a mom, I felt an obligation to his mom. I put myself in DeeDee's shoes and told Amanda that if this had happened to one of my daughters, I would hope that a person would tell me.

After I dropped her off at work, I headed back home and thought more about how to approach DeeDee. No matter how difficult it would be to talk to her about this, I had to do it. I knew DeeDee, but not well. I worried, concerned that maybe she would think I was strange. How should I do this? I couldn't imagine just knocking on their door and saying, "Hi. I saw your son with Jesus on the night he died."

Maybe Amanda was right, I thought. Maybe I shouldn't be telling people I'd had this experience. They could very well think I was crazy.

But I knew in my heart that no matter how strange this might all seem, and no matter how hard it might be, if Jesus and Adam wanted his family to know, I would have to do it. Even at the cost of having people think I was crazy. Until I felt the timing was right to do this, my mind would be working overtime. I pondered the scenarios that could take place when I did speak to them about it, including a door being slammed in my face. Even though David and DeeDee seemed like gentle people, this could be very upsetting for someone who was just beginning the grieving process.

And what about the part about her son becoming famous? What could that possibly have meant? This even sounded strange to me. It didn't make sense that people could be famous in heaven, when I knew we were all equal in God's eyes.

I guess what I questioned the most about the whole thing was why a young man I barely knew had appeared to me the night he died. I sent a prayer to Adam, reasoning that if he could appear to me the night he died, then he could surely let me know what I should do.

"Please, Adam, if you want me to tell your parents about this experience I had, you will have to show me how to do it, and when."

Telling Adam's Mom

(December 16, 2005)

I don't remember why I wasn't working that day. It was during the week, when I would normally be at work. I do remember knowing that would be the day I would speak to Adam's mom. I hadn't been thinking particularly hard on it the night before or anything, but it had come to me that morning. A "knowing" I can't explain.

It wasn't going to be easy. I wasn't even sure how I would go about the whole thing. I only knew this was the day it would happen. It didn't, however, stop me from asking God if maybe I could have something a little easier to do that day.

It was approximately a week before Christmas. I thought maybe I'd bake some Christmas cookies and take them, along with a Christmas card, over to the family. I knew DeeDee would be home, since she made her living by taking care of children in her home. I prayed and, to tell you the truth, talked to Adam all morning. All the way to DeeDee's house, I asked Jesus and Adam to tell me the right things to say.

I knew in my heart that this was what I was supposed to do. But I also knew I could possibly upset his mom. I certainly didn't want to add to the hurt I knew the family was going through. I guess the bottom line was I'd decided to take the chance of someone thinking I was crazy, rather than disappoint Jesus by not delivering His message.

My Mary

With cookies and a card in my hand, off I went to visit DeeDee. She opened the door when I knocked, and though she seemed surprised, she invited me in. As I walked into her living room, the first thing I noticed was a beautiful Bible lying on her coffee table. I commented on it immediately, and she said it had just been delivered to her that morning, sent by the union where Adam had worked. Seeing the Bible gave me courage. It was like confirmation, telling me I was doing the right thing.

We both sat down, and I started right off. "DeeDee," I said, "I don't know why I was given this privilege, but the night Adam died, I saw him with Jesus."

DeeDee began to cry, but nodded with encouragement when she saw I had more to say. I gently told her exactly what had happened that night, and what Jesus had said to me. When I came to the part about Adam becoming famous, I was concerned she would find it difficult to believe. I was having a hard time with it myself.

But she said she believed me. She had been having a really bad day and was missing Adam terribly. She said that by my sharing this with her, I brought her comfort. DeeDee confided in me that Adam never left home without saying goodbye to her first, then she cried even more. When she was more calm, I told her I was confused because my husband had told me he believed Adam had died around nine o'clock, but Adam had appeared to me just after seven o'clock. DeeDee smiled gently and said he died just after seven, but it was nine o'clock by the time they had taken him to the hospital.

I also told DeeDee that I had a very strong feeling Adam was working with children. I don't know why, but this kept coming to me. I laughed and said I would probably be working alongside him when I died, because I love children. Their honesty touches my heart.

"DeeDee," I said, "if, by chance, when we both die, you see me up there working with Adam, I want you to remember this moment." I smiled. "I'll give you a wink and we'll both remember."

Telling Adam's Mom

As I look back now, this makes sense to me. DeeDee had cared for children in her home for all of Adam's life. Adam had always been surrounded by children, and he loved them. It didn't surprise me that he'd been training his whole life so he could do his important job in heaven. I can't imagine a more crucial job than to love and take care of the children in heaven.

> *At that time the disciples came to Jesus and asked, "Who is the greatest in the kingdom of heaven?" He called a child, whom he put among them, and said, "Truly I tell you, unless you change and become like children, you will never enter the kingdom of heaven. Whoever becomes humble like this child is the greatest in the kingdom of heaven. Whoever welcomes one such child in my name welcomes me"* (Matthew 18:1-5).

I, of course, don't know any of this for sure. It's just a strong gut feeling I have. What I do know, though, is that DeeDee said she'd had a dream about Adam the week before my visit. In this dream, he was carrying a small child in his arms. The next day she received a call from one of her close friends, who told DeeDee a little boy she'd known had passed away very suddenly that day.

Some people would call this a coincidence. At one time, I probably would have called it one myself. I no longer believe in coincidences. I now believe everything in life will unfold when it should. Maybe this dream was a beautiful sign from a son to his mom, telling her she'd trained him well for his important job in heaven.

As I was leaving her house that day, DeeDee asked me to write down exactly what Jesus had said to me so I would never forget.

"Patsy," she said, "a few years ago, when I first met you, I sensed there was something different about you."

It was a somewhat surprising statement, but I think sometimes we are given a sixth sense about people. Especially moms,

My Mary

when it comes to our children. Looking back, I wonder if DeeDee had sensed that her oldest son would end up having a spiritual connection with me years later. She couldn't have known that at the time, though.

Walking home from DeeDee's that day, I still didn't understand why I had been chosen for this. I did, however, have a feeling that life, as I'd known it, would never be the same.

I did exactly what DeeDee had asked when I got home. I opened my night table drawer and pulled out the program we'd been given at the funeral, about celebrating Adam's life, and wrote down the three messages I'd received from Jesus. Afterward, as I was closing the drawer with the three messages safely inside, I sent up a little prayer. I prayed I'd brought some comfort to a hurting family, and I hoped that Jesus and Adam were smiling down on me.

Planning of the Rosary Garden

(January 2006)

Before Adam died, his dad, David, had been scheduled to attend a business conference in Florida. DeeDee had been planning to go on this trip with him, but David decided to cancel the trip, because it would be too soon after Adam's death. After much persuasion by David's coworkers, family, and friends, they decided to take the trip. While they were in Florida, they drove by a beautiful church called the Basilica of the National Shrine of Mary, Queen of the Universe. As they were passing, DeeDee suggested to David that they attend a Mass there. So that weekend they did.

After Mass, they took a walk outside and found themselves in a beautiful Rosary Garden. DeeDee told me later that a tremendous peace had come over both her and David while they were in this garden. It also touched their hearts, because their son had such a love for our Blessed Mother. Over the next few years, we came to learn more about the love he'd had for her.

Adam had a great aunt on his mom's side who was a Sister of Charity. They always referred to her as Sister Chris. When Adam was three years old, Sister Chris had given him a plastic statue of the Blessed Mother. The family was amazed by how much Adam loved his little statue. He took her with him whenever he went anywhere. Sometimes DeeDee found the little statue floating in Adam's bath water among all his toy soldiers.

My Mary

Adam's family with Sister Chris

DeeDee shared a sweet story with me about when Adam was younger, after Sister Chris had given him the statue. They had been on vacation and had gone to Ingonish, in Cape Breton. Their two little boys were sitting in the back seat of the car when all of a sudden Adam let out a gasp. They were driving past a church at the side of the road, and he started yelling, "There's my Mary! There's my Mary!"

David turned the car around and pulled into the church parking lot, where they opened the door and let Adam out. The little boy ran to the statue of Mary and wrapped his arms around her.

"My Mary! My Mary!" he exclaimed.

After Adam was diagnosed with cancer, he often stayed in the hospital for chemo or overnight stays. His little statue of our Blessed Mother always went with him. He kept her in his pocket, and when he stayed overnight she stayed with him. Sitting in that Rosary Garden that day, feeling such peace, and knowing their young son had carried such a love for our Blessed Mother, they

Planning of the Rosary Garden

decided to honour their son and his love for Mary. They also wanted to give a gift to their parish community, thanking them for all the support and prayers they'd given the O'Neils while Adam had been sick.

David and DeeDee decided to put a Rosary Garden on the property of the church where they attended Mass. When they

*Patsy in front of Blessed Mother Statue Adam hugged when he was little.
Picture taken at St. Peter's Parish, Ingonish, Nova Scotia*

came home from their trip, they were excited about their plan. They started to talk to people about their idea for the garden, and while people thought it sounded like a wonderful idea, they had no idea how big and beautiful the O'Neils' vision for this garden really was.

First Anniversary of Adam's Death
(November 17, 2006)

As the first anniversary of Adam's death approached, the O'Neil family was on my mind. I wanted to let them know I was thinking about them, and I thought it would be nice if I got them a card and maybe a little something special to go with it. This first anniversary would be a difficult one, and I was having a hard time deciding what would be an appropriate gift. To be honest, I was a bit concerned.

I called one day, just before the anniversary, hoping to speak to DeeDee. When the answering machine clicked on, Adam's name was still on the message, along with those of the rest of the family. I was, at first, shocked to hear that, but my next reaction was one of concern. What if the family wasn't moving on? I knew removing his name would be very painful and would finalize the fact that he wasn't coming back, but by doing so, they would have to face the reality that the family was now three, no longer four.

After my experience with Adam, I took a number of bereavement and palliative workshops. From those I learned that each person's grief is unique. We must respect and accept that what is normal for one family may not be normal for another.

All that week I wondered what I could give the family to help comfort them. Eventually I decided to give them a book. Unfortunately, DeeDee had told me the family had been given many books to read after Adam had died, and although they appreciated this act of kindness from others, they were overwhelmed

My Mary

with so many different books. And yet I still thought a book would be the best gift from me.

A few days before the anniversary, I made a hair appointment with my cousin, John. He is a very spiritual person, and I thought I might ask him if he had any ideas of what I could pick up that might help bring comfort to the family.

When I arrived for my hair appointment, John wasn't there. I waited for a few minutes, reading a magazine, and when I looked up he was coming in the door. He'd been at the bookstore next door. He said he had been waiting for a long time for a specific book to come in and had just gotten a call that morning saying it had finally arrived. I asked if I could see it, because we share a lot of the same interests, and I thought I might enjoy the book as well. He passed me the book, and I stared at the title: *Quit Kissing My Ashes (A Mother's Journey Through Grief)*.

I gawked up at him. "John, I know you just bought this book for yourself, but you actually bought it for me."

He and I have a close relationship, so he wasn't surprised that I said something like that. He did ask me why, though. I told him about DeeDee and Adam, explaining the first anniversary of his death was in a few days. I told him how important it was to me, that I was searching for just the right gift for this anniversary. I also shared with him the experience I'd had the night Adam died. He handed me the book.

I laughed. "Don't worry. I promise I'll buy you another book."

On my way to work the day of the anniversary, I decided to put the gift in their mailbox. I wanted to give them privacy and the opportunity to open the gift by themselves. But as I pulled up in front of their house, I saw DeeDee looking out her front window. It appeared I would have to actually pass her the gift, not drop it off like I had hoped.

I knew this day would be an emotional one for them. My mind spun with thoughts as I climbed the front steps. Oh great, I

First Anniversary of Adam's Death

thought to myself. I'm trying to make her feel better, and now I'm going to make her cry this early in the morning. What I came to realize over the following few years was that DeeDee had a wonderful gift: the gift of tears. I would witness this many times. One day we were at a conference together and just before the speaker got up, DeeDee's friend, Rae, passed her a handful of Kleenex. DeeDee, and those of us sitting with her, couldn't help but laugh.

When DeeDee opened the door, I passed her the gift and gave her a hug. I told her I wanted to acknowledge Adam's first anniversary and let them know that I cared.

"I have to tell you," I admitted over my shoulder, already walking back to my car, "I didn't find the gift. It found me."

My hope was that the book would bring them some type of comfort. I was pleased that after DeeDee read it, she said it had. That's really all we can do when people are in pain: let them know we care. That night, when I thought about how the gift had come to be, I smiled and sent a little prayer to Adam. There was no doubt in my mind that he had chosen the gift for the first anniversary of his passing. I believe he wanted to make sure his family knew they had his blessing to move forward with their healing.

I was thankful I had trusted those whispers and knocked on DeeDee's door so many months before.

As the anniversary of the death of a loved one draws near, it is accompanied by many emotions. Sometimes it can be a painful reminder of who is missing in a person's life. Some people use this date to do something special to remember the loved one.

We are all very different when it comes to our own grief journey. The most important thing is to follow what your heart tells you is right for you and your family.

That was exactly what the O'Neils did. The night Adam passed away, he was doing what he loved, hanging out with his friends and playing football. On the Saturday following every anniversary of

My Mary

Adam's death, his family and friends still celebrate his life with a football game. They even have a large cup for the winning team.

After the game is over, the cup is filled with a spirited drink. Every member of the winning team takes a drink and sends up a cheer to Adam, then every member of the other team does the same. When the cup is empty, one of the members of the winning team gets to take it home until the next year.

Picture of the football game played in memory of Adam each year on the Saturday, following the anniversary of his death with friends and family

This togetherness brings comfort to the people attending. It's their way of remembering a young man who was full of life and love. Afterward, they all head out and enjoy brunch as a group. Even though he's no longer with them, they are thankful for the time when he was an active part of their lives. They are thankful for their own memories of Adam, which each of them cherishes in their own way.

In the Garden with Jesus

(November 25, 2006)

When a person goes for a massage, it's supposed to be relaxing. When I went, I certainly didn't expect to close my eyes and find myself in a garden, sitting at Jesus's feet. But that's exactly what I saw.

The whole time I was being massaged, I sat at His feet, listening intently. Strangely enough, I don't know what He was telling me, because He wasn't speaking the same way He had when He'd appeared to me with Adam. This time He spoke directly to my heart. What I did understand was that the words He was giving me were important for me to hear. What a beautiful experience, being able to spend time with such a gentle teacher.

When the massage was over, so was the vision. When you experience something like this, it's hard to shift back into the rat race of the real world. You try to hang on to the feeling for as long as you can. But the reality is we're here to make a difference in the world, and most times that takes hard work.

Looking back now, I believe the reason Jesus appeared to me was that for many years I had been telling him I was ready to do His work. Whatever He wanted me to do. I'd thought I was ready to take on any task He might ask of me. What I didn't understand at the time, was that in order for me to do the work He would be asking of me, I first had to do some healing myself. Before I could help others who were hurting, I had to heal my own wounds.

My Mary

In truth, I didn't even know I had healing to do. I thought I was just fine the way I was. I figured, despite all the pain I had experienced in my life, I still turned out to be a caring, loving human being. Most times, however, human beings bury their pain down so deep we think it's gone. Unfortunately, when we least expect it, it will find a way to wriggle back up to the surface. Since our Father is omniscient, He knew I would have to go back to this vision He'd given me at the massage therapist's. I would need to draw from this experience, use it to help me get though all the buried pain that was now rising in me.

My pain came from the loss of three very important people in my life. By the time I was twenty-five, I had lost my dad, my mom, and my nan. At the time, it had seemed easier to just get on with life. It was probably easier for me to cope that way.

Now, years later, I had to start my healing process. I have discovered that when you experience the deaths of three people you love, you need to relive those memories in order to heal. You can imagine how painful this can be. It all came flooding back, and the pain felt unbearable. On one day in particular I felt so overwhelmed by emotion, I got on my knees to pray, tears streaming down my face. I don't think I'd done that since I was a little girl.

"I don't know if I can do this anymore, Jesus. It's too painful!" I cried.

But no matter how much it hurt, I could still hear Jesus saying to me, "I know how painful this is for you, Patsy, but you need to heal in order to do what I'm asking of you."

When I'm reading this section again, an image comes to mind. It's a cartoon of a man carrying a cross. He keeps asking Jesus to cut it shorter for him, even though other people are carrying the same size cross as he has. Jesus cuts it down for him, but the man keeps asking Him to cut it some more. Jesus does this for him, and the man thanks him. They all keep walking until they arrive at a ravine.

Everyone uses their crosses to help them pass over the ravine, but this gentleman's cross is now too short.

Such a powerful cartoon, and so true. We all have our crosses to bear. We should probably learn to ask God what we are meant to learn from a rough situation, instead of asking Him to remove it entirely. I made a decision that day. I was determined to carry that heavy cross, but I asked if He would please walk beside me while I did it. I knew how much He loved me. I also knew in my heart that He was waiting for me to ask Him.

Sometimes when I'm praying to God and having a conversation with him, the answer seems to materialize right before my eyes. I really am thankful for times like this. One day I went out walking, and I was very upset. I asked God why I had to go through all this emotional turmoil and pain, when all I wanted to was to do His work. I stomped through the rest of my walk, listening to nothing but the anger in my head.

When I got home, I turned on my computer and opened my email. For about six months before this, I had been receiving St. Therese quotes daily. I read them every day, but most of the time they really didn't touch my heart. When I opened this particular quote, my heart actually bloomed with emotion when I read it.

> *"How I would like to make you understand the tenderness of the Heart of Jesus, what He is asking of you"* (St. Therese of Lisieux, the Little Flower).

From that little reminder, I understood that Jesus didn't want me to hurt. It's just that sometimes we have to go through painful experiences in order to understand what He is really asking of us.

It didn't take long for me to understand what was being asked of me. The whispers became louder. "Comfort My people."

One thing about grief that I understand because of my own experience is that if you don't take the time to grieve when you do lose someone you love, it will catch up to you. You'll be going along in your life and something will trigger that deeply buried pain.

Today's world gives a person a very short window of time in which to grieve the loss of someone they love. Then they are expected to just get on with life, proceed as they had before. But we must not forget that the death of someone you love changes your life forever. You now have a new identity you must learn. It takes time to adjust.

If we want to be able to help people who are experiencing the loss of a loved one, we need to allow them to experience this loss in their own unique way. We need to have patience and show understanding with them. By allowing them to go through all or at least some of the different stages of grief, it will help them experience their new life in a more meaningful way.

Death Is a Natural Process

If death is such a natural process, why does it hurt so much to lose a loved one? I don't know how you were brought up, but in my family, we didn't sit around and discuss death. A lot of people ignore the subject, so we don't really get to understand that death is a natural part of the living process. Instead, it becomes something that we fear.

I believe the existence of support groups is a blessing. Most times the groups help people go through the grief process. Until they can finally heal, the sufferers can at least find help in regaining some type of normalcy in their lives. When it had been my time to grieve, I hadn't even known these groups existed.

Our heart never seems to be prepared for death. Sometimes, even after our loved one has suffered with a long illness, we struggle with different emotions. One of the most difficult emotions is the sensation of emptiness. When we realize we can never again experience our loved one's presence, we feel empty.

One factor that influences the way we react to grief is our religious background. At first we may be angry at God for taking away our loved one. After a while we turn to Him when we hurt, and He gives us the strength to trust. God shares the hurt in our hearts. He will walk with us on this journey if we open our hearts to Him. If we allow ourselves to spend time with Him in prayer, we will begin to hear His whispers. Eventually, although I miss my loved ones who have passed, I found comfort in knowing that they are with Jesus. Although I can't see them physically, I know I will always have a sacred connection and spiritual bond with them. Not even death can sever the bond I have with them.

As I share each of my own experiences about the deaths of my loved ones, you'll see how each loss was unique. I am fortunate, because my faith helped me to accept their deaths more easily than if I hadn't believed in the afterlife.

Dad

I turned thirteen the month before my dad passed away, dying very unexpectedly, suffering complications from a fall. Within a few days of his fall, he was gone.

I am named after my dad, whose name was Patrick. My mom told me that as soon as he saw me in the hospital after I was born, he asked her to name me after him because he thought I looked so much like him. A short while later, I was baptized Patricia. For all of my young life, I had an extremely close relationship with my dad. He had owned a candy store, with a restaurant attached. I could always be found behind the counter, working with him.

The day he fell, I was home from school. I remember very clearly that I was sitting in his favourite chair when I heard a crashing noise. I didn't go upstairs right away, but when I did, he was being lifted onto a stretcher. They put him in an ambulance, and I stood at the roadside, watching through tears as the ambulance drove away with my dad inside. I was very scared.

I was shocked when my mom told me he'd fallen on his way back to work, tripping over only three steps we had leading outside our house. A few days after his fall, my cousin Jenny and I went to the hospital, wanting to see him. We had a little visit, and I remember rubbing lotion on his elbows for him. My uncle came in afterward to visit Dad, so Jenny and I had to leave. I said goodbye, and he smiled at me. That was the last time I saw him.

I wish my family had shown more open affection as I'd been growing up. When I eventually created my own family, it was important that we all were able to demonstrate our affection for each other. I am thankful that my last memory of my dad is of our smiling at each other, but how much more wonderful it would have been if the last time I'd seen him I had shown my love more openly. If only I could have left him with a kiss and a hug.

I will never forget the night my dad died. My mom had been visiting him at the hospital, and I saw her walk into the house along with my seventeen-year-old sister, Debbie, and her boyfriend. Mom looked haggard and unfocused, like a zombie. She wore no expression, and she stared straight ahead. I realize now that she was probably in shock, but at that moment the only thing I understood was everything in my world had turned upside down. I walked towards her, but she didn't see me. I remember asking my sister if Dad was okay, but I was afraid of the answer. I was thirteen. I didn't want my life to change.

She told me he'd died, and my heart dropped. Inside my head I was screaming, "Not my daddy! Please God, don't take him away from us!"

At the same time, my little sisters were calling my name from their bedroom. I had two younger sisters: Leona, who was eight at the time, and Evelyn, who was a year older than Leona. I headed to their room and could tell right away that they had heard the conversation, and they were scared.

"Patsy, did Daddy die?" they asked.

Everything in me wished this was just a nightmare, and I'd wake up any minute. But it wasn't, and they needed to know the truth. Those scared little faces looked up at me, and I begin to cry.

"Yes. He died tonight," I whispered.

My Mary

That night was an awful beginning for me. Now I had responsibilities a thirteen-year-old should never have been given.

My mom was never the same after that. Even though I had an older sister, I was told by the remaining adults in my life that I would now have the responsibility of running the household. My mom wasn't coping, and that was just the way it had to be. Now I'd lost my dad, whom I had loved so much, and I was about to lose my childhood as well. At the time, I didn't even question it. I was trying to cope with not having a father anymore and had to adjust to all the changes in my life.

Two things stand out in my mind with regards to the wake and the funeral. When my sisters and I were brought into the wake, we saw my dad for the first time after he'd died. We stopped at the doorway before we went inside, and I remember looking in the room, seeing my dad lying so still in the casket. My mom knelt on the floor next to the casket, sobbing uncontrollably. I didn't want to go in.

The other thing that stands out in my mind was how many people attended the funeral. My dad was a business man, and he was well known in the community. I remember leaving the church, following the casket, and looking at all the people through the sheen of my tears. They all wore a look of such sadness, and their expressions touched something in my heart that I will never forget. My dad had been in the army years earlier, so when they were burying him that day, the men from the Legion played the Last Post. I still think of my dad every time I hear this piece, and it brings tears to my eyes.

To this day, I find goodbyes so difficult. My one regret about my dad's passing, and the thing that was the hardest for me, was that I never got to say a real goodbye to him. I never got to tell him how much I loved him and would miss him. I would have wanted him to know that because of the thirteen years I'd had him in my life, I would work really hard to grow up into a daughter of whom he would be proud.

Losing anyone we love is extremely hard. With my dad, I found it very difficult, since I had no time to prepare myself. Because of the shock of losing him so suddenly, it took a very long time before I could accept the fact that he was never coming back. No matter how much crying or bargaining I did with God, I couldn't change the fact that at the end of the day there was still an empty chair at our kitchen table.

Nan

For about a year before I turned nineteen, I knew my nan's health was failing. I was living away from home at the time, and when I came home for Christmas that year, she asked me to come back home to live. I believe she knew her time left with us was very short. She wanted the reassurance that I would be close by and able to watch over my younger sisters.

My nan, who was as petite as a person could be, was the "rock" of her family. She was tiny, but strong. None of her family members messed with her. When I was about two years old, she came to live with my family, helping to take over my mother's role. I don't think this helped my mom with learning how to take responsibility, but Nan's grandchildren were so lucky. She loved us all very much.

Nan was the only grandparent my sisters knew. Years before, it seems there had been more emphasis on spending family time together. Every Sunday, Nan's brothers and sisters came to visit her, reminiscing for hours about their growing up years. What a blessing it was to be part of this! They didn't have long chats with us kids, but it gave us a sense of how important it was to keep in touch with family members.

My Mary

We all loved Nan so much. I slept with her for many years when I was a little girl, and we had a very close relationship. I cannot imagine our life without her, because the reality is if she hadn't lived with us after my dad died, there is a great possibility we wouldn't have been able to stay together as a family. Nan was the glue that held us together. Although we didn't speak of it, we all knew that was the truth.

My nan had a strong faith. It gave me comfort to see her trust this faith when everything was falling apart. Through watching her, I learned that God will always be there for us. No matter what, we can always count on Him to get us through our trials.

At one point my ailing nan decided that I was the only one who knew how to turn her when she needed to change position. She was so little at that time, with very little weight left on her. I always felt badly when she had to be turned. I knew how painful the movement was for her. But sharing this special time with her gave me the opportunity at an earlier age to experience what it was like to spend time with someone who was dying.

One day she told me she was finding it harder and harder to keep living. This was extremely difficult for me to hear, let alone understand, at age nineteen. I couldn't imagine that someone wouldn't want to keep living. I understand better now. It wasn't that she didn't want to live. She had worked hard all her life, caring for her family, and now she was too tired to keep going.

I believe she hung on as long as she did for all of us. I was afraid of losing her. I knew she kept my mom on track. I also knew that when she passed, life was going to get even harder for us. I understood it was difficult for her to leave us, and perhaps even more difficult for us to lose her, but she deserved to rest.

The night she lay dying, I sat with her, reminiscing about how we used to watch our favourite shows together. She had very little strength left, but I held so many beautiful memories of her in her healthier days. Every once in a while she looked at me and pointed to the ceiling. I kept asking her if the light was bothering her, but she shook her head, saying no. Much later, I realized what she was trying to tell me. She was pointing towards heaven. I wish I'd known at that time what she meant, because that would have given me an opportunity to talk about heaven.

I just didn't have enough experience at the time. I stayed awake as long as I could that night, even introducing myself to coffee, to make sure I didn't sleep. I wanted to make sure I was with her when she took her last breath.

When I couldn't keep my eyes open another moment, I told my aunt I needed to lay down for half an hour, then I'd go back to sit with Nan. It seemed as if I had just laid my head on the pillow and was drifting off, when my aunt gently shook me awake. I remember looking up at her and seeing such sadness in her eyes.

"Patsy, she's gone," she whispered.

I jumped up in a panic and ran to Nan's room. She can't be gone! I screamed in my head. I couldn't accept that she was gone. I kept telling my family they were wrong, kept swearing she was still breathing.

Finally my older sister, Debbie, grabbed me and shook me by my shoulders. I think I was beginning to frighten them. As she held me, I felt my body go stiff with shock. I knew I was becoming hysterical, but I couldn't stop myself.

She slapped my face and shouted, "Patsy, she's dead! Stop it! She's not breathing."

I collapsed on the floor and cried my heart out. Even though I knew it was her time, I didn't want to let her go. I was afraid. I believed we still needed her. But what she needed was for us to let her go.

Nan died in our home, which gave me an entirely different experience with death. We got to spend time with her before she

My Mary

died. What a gift this was for me, since I hadn't been able to properly say goodbye to my dad. We had a lot of family members around at the time, and I witnessed firsthand how each of my relatives reacted to the loss. They wanted to be with her until she died, needing to say their own goodbyes in their own way.

Nan was more than just my family's rock. She had four sons and two daughters with families of their own. She was the mother figure for all of us. Everyone listened when Nan spoke, and it was out of respect more than fear.

Out of everyone in my life, I looked up to Nan the most. I learned how to become a strong woman just by watching her. She left me with a beautiful gift: the knowledge that if you have a strong faith, it will get you through anything that life throws at you. I was nineteen when she died, and since then it's amazing how many times I've relied on my faith when life became almost too hard to bear. I only ever knew one grandparent, but I was blessed with having such a beautiful person for a grandparent, and that's all I needed.

I don't remember anything about her wake or funeral. It's almost as if I didn't attend. I think it was just so painful for me to let her go that my mind blocked it out.

She passed away in April. In June of that same year, I met my future husband, Peter. It was love at first sight for me. Not only did I have a physical attraction to him, but he was mature for his age, which was important to me. I also knew right from the start that he was a gentle soul.

I believe Nan picked him out for me after she died. I used to tell people this from time to time, and they would laugh. But in my heart, I believed it was true. Years later, I was at an angel workshop and the lady, Karen, who gave the workshop was walking around the room giving messages to people. She said they were from our angels. She stopped when she got to me, and she smiled.

"The angels are telling me your marriage was made in heaven," she said. "Do you know what this means?"

I couldn't help but chuckle. "Actually," I said, "I do. After my Nan died, I think she picked my husband out for me."

Everyone laughed, and I just kept smiling. Thanks, Nan. You did a great job!

Mom

As I go to write about my mom, the song "A Mother's Love Is a Blessing," is playing in my head. As I said earlier, my mom was never really the same after my dad died. I understood this better once I became a mother. I can see now that she was very dependent on my father. When he died, Dad left four children and a business behind. She tried to keep going, but it was almost too much for her.

As a thirteen-year-old, all I knew was that I had a dad whom I loved dearly, and he'd died. Up until that point, I'd had, from what I can recall, a normal thirteen-year-old life. Then, within a matter of days, I no longer had a father, and I became the adult. Not a role I would have chosen, but one I accepted.

One day I had a conversation with my best friend, Glenna. We had met in our first year of high school. For some reason, we began talking about my growing up years. Glenna was shocked and very upset by what I told her. She couldn't get over the fact that even though she'd been my best friend for years, she had no idea of how much responsibility I'd had at home in my teenage years.

The more I spoke about my younger years, the more her tears fell. When I look back on it, I can see it was actually a beautiful moment: one friend telling of her pain, and the other friend having so much empathy it brought tears to her eyes.

One thing Glenna couldn't understand was why I wasn't bitter and upset with my mom for putting me in that position. At that

My Mary

time I didn't understand it myself, but I never felt anger towards my mom. I tried to carry on the appearance of having normal adolescent years and was helped along by the fact that the group I met in high school didn't live in the same area as I did. They didn't know much about my family. Glenna told me that she'd thought my life was as carefree as hers. I was glad to hear that, because in spite of all the turmoil in my life, I wasn't willing to use any of it as an excuse not to have a normal teenage life.

Patsy and her Mom on her wedding day, March 27, 1982

Death Is a Natural Process

I understood at an early age that you are the one responsible for setting the stage for your life. Just because my home life wasn't an easy one, it didn't mean I wouldn't try to live the best life I could.

I had just turned twenty-three when Peter and I got married. I wished my dad could have walked me down the aisle, and that my nan could have seen me in my wedding dress. I was thankful though, that Mom was a part of my big day.

It was a concern of mine at the time, because a few weeks before my wedding, I told her she needed to go see her doctor. She had a bad cough that just wouldn't go away. She was a smoker, but she'd never had a cough like this before. I kept busy with the wedding plans, but in the back of my mind I was worried about her.

A few days before the wedding, she finally went to see her doctor. He told her he was sending her to Halifax for further testing. I had been living in Cape Breton and was moving to Halifax the day after I was married, so I was happy Peter and I would be there when she came for her testing.

I started a new job in the banking industry the week after I got married. The next week, my mom came up for her appointment with the specialist. She was very nervous, and said if the news was bad she didn't want them to tell her. I was afraid too, but I knew at least one of us would have to be brave.

She stayed in the hospital while they were doing all the tests. When I spoke to her nurse, I asked her to please put in my mom's chart that if the diagnosis was bad, to call me first. I explained that my mom was afraid and believed it was important for me to be with her if they had to give her bad news.

As we all know, life doesn't always unfold as you'd like it to. Here I was, newly married the week before, starting a new job, and living in a new city. When I was called to the phone at work, my heart dropped. No one would be calling me at my new job unless

My Mary

it was bad news. Everyone knew I was working with cash and wouldn't be able to come to the phone that easily.

When I picked up the phone, I heard my mom sobbing. The doctors had just been in, and they had told her she had probably six months to live. My biggest fear had come true: she'd been alone when they'd told her.

"Oh my dear Jesus," I thought, "why does everything have to be so hard? How much does one person have to take? Do You really think I'm that strong? Are You trying to break me?"

I was so frustrated and so angry with God. It seemed no matter how hard I tried to live a good life, blocks were always being put up before me. They say God doesn't give a person more than they can handle, but it's very difficult to believe that when we are in the midst of so much pain. Not only would I have to come to terms with my mom's terminal illness, but I had a new worry: how could I be there for her and my younger sisters when I had just moved to a new location?

When I look back now, I understand He was making me stronger. I was being molded into who He wanted me to be.

Mom was only fifty-one when she was diagnosed. She had been ten years younger than my dad, so both of them had been in their early fifties when they died. When patients are diagnosed with a terminal illness, doctors can give them an estimated time that they think they have to live. In the end, though, it will be God's decision. That day in the hospital when my mom was given the bad news, she was told she probably had six months left to live. At that time she was so petite and frail, it was difficult to imagine she could last that long. But my mom didn't pass away until two years and four months after her diagnosis. The human spirit is absolutely amazing.

I wanted to buy her something she could keep with her, because I couldn't be with her all the time. I hoped she would think of me whenever she looked at it and know how much I loved her. On one of my visits home, I bought her a plastic statue of the Blessed Mother, probably similar to Adam's little statue, except it was bigger. In the back of it I tucked some cloth roses. I found comfort in believing Mary would watch over her since I couldn't.

My heart felt so heavy every time Mom asked me if she was going to be okay. I knew she wanted to hear me say "yes," even though the doctors had told her illness was terminal. I really don't know; maybe this helped her hang on longer.

After this experience, I understood how hard it can be on the family when a person refuses to accept that they are dying. At least if they accept it, you can discuss as a family and learn what your loved one's final wishes are. There may be things you want to say to them, but because of the fear of upsetting them, you keep your thoughts to yourself.

I was lucky, being married to such an understanding man. He knew it was hard for me to live so far away from Mom after she was diagnosed. Living away seemed to make everything worse, in the worrying sense. If I'd been with her, I would have known exactly what was going on. Since I didn't, my imagination ran wild, especially in the still of the night. Peter promised that he would take me home as often as possible, so every second weekend we got in the car and made the trip home to check on her.

As the end of Mom's life approached, I found it even harder to live away. I wanted to be with her all the time. By this time, my youngest sister had come to live with us. One night I received a call saying Mom had been anointed. The hospital staff told my family they didn't think she would last much longer. The next day we headed home, but after a couple of days, she seemed to bounce back. She wasn't going without a fight.

Sadly, I knew her next fight would be her last. That was when I began to have nightmares. In the dreams I couldn't make it home in time to be with her when she died. This helpless feeling plagued me. I began to pray my heart out whenever I had the chance.

"Please God, I wasn't there to say goodbye to my dad, and you took Nan shortly after I left her room. Please let me be with my mom when she dies."

Every time the phone rang, I was afraid it would be the dreaded call. I told Peter it would break my heart if she died without my being there.

The hospital called again, and my sister and I boarded a plane that evening, then went straight to the hospital to see Mom. She seemed to be holding her own, but we could see she was finally losing her battle. Shortly afterward, she lost consciousness. My aunt and older sister said they would take the night shift, sitting by Mom's bed. My younger sisters and I would relieve them in the morning.

The next morning they called from the hospital, saying they were on their way home. "She's not doing great," they told us, "but she could hang on for a few more days."

My sisters and I headed out the door. By the time we arrived at the hospital, her breathing was shallower. After a couple of hours, we noticed that even though she was unconscious, she began to move around a bit. I stood by her bed and my sisters sat in the bed right next to hers, and we all watched with amazement.

With her eyes still closed, Mom held out her frail arms and began talking in a very low whisper. I leaned over to hear the words she was saying, and I thought I heard her say, "I'm ready."

When my sisters asked who she was talking to, I told them I believed someone from the other side was there to take her. My youngest sister was extremely upset, but I kept my eyes on Mom while I tried to calm my sister. Shortly after that, Mom took two little breaths and was gone.

The feeling of peace that passed through my body at that time was wonderful. Otherworldly. It's not easy to watch someone you

Death Is a Natural Process

love when they are dying. Your heart is filled with mixed emotions. You don't want them to suffer, nor do you want to face never seeing them again.

Sometimes people ask what the defining moment was that changed your life. The moment that put you on the path you are on right now.

For me, that moment arrived when Jesus gave me the gift for which I'd prayed so hard. He knew that by giving me this gift it would touch something deep in my heart, and He would be able to use my experiences years later, when He knew I was ready to help bring comfort to His people.

I was relieved that Mom was finally at peace after all those years of struggling. And the thought of someone coming from the other side to meet her gave me such comfort.

I pressed the call bell after she died. The nurse came in and glanced at me, then she looked at Mom.

"She gone," I said.

The nurse checked her pulse. "Yes, she is," she replied.

I called home to tell the rest of my family that Mom had died, then we went to find my cousin who worked in the hospital, so we could tell her as well.

When we met up, Martina looked at me and said, "Your mom died, didn't she?"

I nodded, then asked her how she knew.

"Patsy, the look of peace that's on your face is unbelievable."

Years later, I bought a spiritual CD. When I played one of the songs on it, I was reminded of the night I'd been with my mom when she died.

Referring to Jesus, the lyrics said, "I am the peace this world cannot give."

I know the peace she was singing about. I was blessed to have experienced it on the day my mom died.

My Mary

Eleven months later, I experienced that same sense of peace again. I was three months pregnant with my older daughter, Melissa, and Peter and I had gone away for the weekend with some of our friends. In the morning when we got up, I felt a strong urge to go down to the water. All of our friends had been sitting around, and I got to my feet and told them I would be back shortly. Once I was down by the water, I sat. All of a sudden, a feeling of peace passed through my whole body. I didn't want to move for fear it would end.

Later that day, Peter and I got in the car and headed home. After we'd been driving for a while, I turned to Peter. "Someone died," I said.

"Who?" he asked.

I shrugged. "I just know someone I'm close to has died."

We didn't have cell phones back then, so the moment we stepped into our house I called my family to make sure everything was all right. My heart beat a little faster as I dialed. I recognized the voice as my sister answered the phone.

In the background, someone asked, "Did you tell her?"

My Uncle Dode, with whom I was very close, had died that day from a massive heart attack. He had been the one to fill in for my dad and walk me down the aisle at my wedding.

My family suggested that I not go home for the funeral, because I was pregnant. They thought the experience would be too hard on me, and I knew they were right. So I didn't go. This was my first pregnancy, and everything about it was new to me. I didn't want to take any chances or do anything that might harm my baby.

After my mom died, I began to have what some people call "strange experiences." I remember someone in the family referring to me one time as a "white witch." My best friend, Glenna, bought me a dream dictionary. Inside she wrote that she didn't want me to tell her anything I dreamt about her, unless, of course, it was good.

I can't explain it, but it was almost like my intuition became stronger on the night my mom died. I started to sense things that I'd never noticed in the past.

Three deaths of family members, three different experiences. Sometimes I'm asked which of these deaths was the hardest for me. I loved them all dearly, but I believe the hardest for me was the death of my dad. We'd been so close, and I was so young when he'd died. Not being given the opportunity to say goodbye was a pain I carried in my heart for many years to come.

Camille

When my husband was turning fifty in July 2009, I asked him what he would like us to do for his birthday. He didn't want to have a big party to celebrate, but he liked my idea of taking his mom around the Cabot Trail in Cape Breton. The Cabot Trail is a beautiful area, and spending a few days in a country cottage would give us some quiet time together.

Looking back, I can see that trip was a blessing. Considering the turmoil that would consume the next four months of our lives, it was a gift that he and his mom got to spend a few days relaxing and enjoying the country air. The day we came back from Cape Breton, Peter got a call that his sister, Camille, who was a year older than he was, had landed in Emergency. Camille was a carpenter and the only sister to five brothers. There weren't a lot of women in that trade when she entered it, so she had to be tough, putting up with the men with whom she worked. She was proud to work in a profession that included so few women.

For her this was the first of many trips to an emergency room. Four months from that date, Camille lost her battle with cancer.

By the time Camille got sick, I'd probably been a volunteer in palliative care and bereavement for two years. I had spent time with

My Mary

a lot of dying people by then. It's different though, when it's your own family. It is very hard to watch the person you love go through the pain of losing a sibling.

I've heard before that often the way you die reflects how you lived. With Camille this couldn't have been more true. Tough up until the very end, she would not accept her diagnosis. When Peter called his two brothers and told them she had been given a terminal diagnosis, she told them it wasn't true.

The next day, after she was released from the hospital, Peter brought her to our house for a while, saying one of his other brothers would pick her up a couple of hours later. This gave me an opportunity to be alone with her. It was a beautiful day outside, so we sat, drinking tea on our back deck. That afternoon, Camille admitted to me that she didn't want to die. With tears streaming down her face, she said she wanted to live to be at least in her seventies. Through my own tears, I told Camille, as gently as I could, that we would have to trust God on this.

She also said that ever since she'd gone into the hospital, she'd felt her dad around her. Duke had drowned thirteen-and-a-half years before that, so the family had never gotten to say goodbye to him. I asked her if it gave her comfort, knowing she could feel him around her. She smiled and said it did. Talking with Camille brought back memories of when my own mom was dying, because they'd both been in denial. Camille could be very stubborn. She told her family repeatedly that she wasn't dying. Sometimes she got very angry about the prognosis.

The Christmas before Camille died, Peter's mom came for a trip from Cape Breton to spend Christmas with us. This gave Peter a wonderful opportunity to have his mom, sister, two brothers, and other family members over for Christmas dinner. It wasn't too long before I began taking pictures. After a while, I think I was getting on everyone's nerves, but I wouldn't stop. I remember laughing and saying, "Just wait, you guys, someday you'll be glad I took all these pictures."

We ended up using some of those pictures for the newspaper announcement of Camille's death, as well as in the funeral program. I was glad that Peter's family had pictures of themselves with her that they could treasure.

Sometimes, even in death, it's important to find humour. In May, we got together for Camille's interment in Cape Breton. Her wish had been that her ashes be buried in the Bras d'Or Lakes. After the ceremony was over, I took the camera out again, thinking it wasn't that often that Peter's family had an opportunity to all be together at once.

I heard someone say, "Oh no. Here comes Patsy with that camera again. Which one of us will be next?"

It was a laugh we all needed after saying a final goodbye to their only sister and Irene's only daughter.

Sometimes when I tell people how hard it was on the family when Camille wouldn't accept her terminal illness, they suggest this was her way of coping and say we should have let her carry on that way. But there's more to think about than just coping. When people haven't gone through their own experience with this type of situation, they sometimes don't realize that when a woman has been independent her whole life, has never been married or had children, there has to be someone who will take care of all the legal matters that come with death. Camille had her own house, and we never knew any of her financial business. We weren't sure if she even had a will or insurance to cover any debt she might have owed. This is the reality side of death the survivors are left to deal with.

In a fantasy world, it's easy to say, "just let her pretend she's not dying."

This doesn't work in the real world. As Camille became sicker and sicker and still wouldn't discuss her death, the family had to make a decision. They decided one of them would have to approach her about the topic, and in the end it was decided that person would be Peter. He told me after he came home that night that it had been one of the hardest things he'd ever had to do. It tore at his heart, and both of them ended up crying. He did have a valuable conversation with her, and in the end she agreed to sign whatever they needed her to sign, making things easier on them.

Another important issue that comes up when people are dying is finding out how they would want to be honoured when they died. We all had our own ideas about what we thought Camille might like, but these were our ideas, not hers. This wasn't an easy subject for Peter to bring up, since Camille wouldn't talk about dying, so as we got closer to the end of her life, we decided I would be the one to talk to her about this.

Early one Saturday morning, Peter and I set out for Camille's house in the country. The hour-long drive gave us time to talk about how we would approach this difficult task. We decided Peter would occupy himself by doing work in her yard, and when she and I were alone, I would talk to her about her wishes. Death is never an easy subject to bring up. Especially if the person isn't ready to accept that they're dying. No matter how hard it was to have this conversation with her, I felt in my heart that I had an obligation to Camille as a sister-in-law. It was important that we made sure we did things the way she wanted.

I tried to be as gentle as I could, but I also had to be realistic and get some answers. This conversation would make things easier for the family in the long run. Camille was brought up Catholic, though she wasn't the type of person you would find at Mass every Sunday. Over the years, she and I had many conversations about our faith and spiritual beliefs. She believed she didn't necessarily have to be in a church to be close to Jesus. She often told me that in hard times—and she'd had more than most—it was Jesus who got her through them.

Camille also had a love of angels. She had many of them scattered around her house. She told me when she spent time in nature, that was when she felt closest to the angels. Our love of angels was something she and I had in common. I asked her if she would want a Catholic funeral, and I was somewhat surprised when the answer was an emphatic yes. I guess I'd figured since she wasn't in church all the time, this wouldn't be as important to her.

This was a great lesson for me: we really don't know what's in others' hearts. We may think we know, but only God really knows. I asked her in which Catholic church she would want her funeral, and there was no hesitation when she told me it should be St. Mary's Cathedral Basilica, in Halifax. She thought it was the most beautiful church she'd ever been in. Being a carpenter, the church's architectural artistry was important to her. She also wished to be cremated and said she would like her ashes to be put in the Bras d'Or Lakes. She wanted to be brought back to Cape Breton, where she'd grown up.

By now tears were falling down both our faces. "Camille," I said, "it's so strange you mentioned the Basilica."

I told her that I always carpool from work, but the day before this conversation had taken place, I had to take the bus home. It had travelled a different route from the usual way I go home. Because the traffic was so backed up, it stopped in front of the Basilica. I looked out the window of the bus, staring at the church, remembering that I had been inside it numerous times. My cousin John Maynard was one of its parishioners, and we had attended Mass with him there. That day, as I sat in the bus, I was thinking how beautiful the church was. I promised I would do everything I could so that she could have her funeral in that church.

My Mary

One day Peter visited Camille in the hospital, and she asked him to take her outside. Peter pushed Camille's wheelchair out the doorway and as they came up the corridor, Peter saw our parish priest, Fr. Ron, who stopped to chat with them. When I arrived at the hospital that night, she mentioned she had met Fr. Ron that afternoon. She thought he had a good heart and a great sense of humour.

Fr. Ron ended up being the priest who did Camille's service. I believe she would have been pleased that he was the one. Camille had always laughed a lot, and she loved people with a great sense of humour.

We made arrangements, with the help of my cousin, to have Camille's funeral at the Basilica. All of her family members worked hard to ensure her farewell honoured her. I sat with Irene, Camille's mom, when she was trying to pick the readings for the funeral. There was no question that the front of the program would need an angel on it.

"Irene," I said, "we need to find a poem to put on the front with this angel."

I sat at the computer, trying to find that perfect poem for the program, but was having no luck at all. Sometimes in our lives, things fall into place, but not until they are supposed to. I got up to get something from the living room, and as I was bending over, a book caught my eye.

Months before, I'd visited my friend Martha. As I was leaving, she passed me a book. "I think you'd really enjoy this book," she said. "Why don't you borrow it for a while?"

It was a book on angel poems. I took it home and read it, placed it in my book rack, and completely forgot about it. Now it had found me again. I came out of the living room, holding the book in my hand.

"Look what I found! Or should I say...look what found me!" I let the book fall open, and when I read the poem on that page, tears came to my eyes.

Angels Are Watching

Do they sit and watch us, these angels of which we are unaware?
Heads on their hands, and peek at our world?
I think I can see them sometimes,
if I look up and squint really hard.
I think I can hear them sometimes:
celestial murmurs that accompany our
hardships and will one day lead us home.

"Angels: Heavenly Blessings"
Carol Smith

Camille had told me she talked to her angels, and after reading this I had no doubt that they'd heard every word she said. They were with her through all her hardships, and they were with her when she died, so they could lead her home.

I worked hard making sure everything was the way the family would want her remembered. As I was working in the kitchen that morning, Camille's face kept coming to my mind. The day before she'd died, I'd gone to visit her on my lunch hour. I worked at the hospital next door, so it was close by. As I was leaving, I tried to cheer her up before I left. I can't remember what I said, but it was something that made her smile. As I looked at her face, the sun was just coming in the window, and the light shone on her face, looking as if her whole face had lit up.

She gave me a big smile, and said, "Thank you, Patsy."

That was the last time I saw Camille conscious. Now, standing in my quiet kitchen, I could feel her presence. I couldn't get her smile, and the way the sun had been shining on her face, out of my mind. I heard her voice again, saying, "Thank you, Patsy."

She left me with a beautiful gift. She knew I would do everything I could to help make this a beautiful memory for her loved ones. That whole day, every time I pictured her smiling face and thought of her thank you, my eyes filled up with tears.

But by the end of the day, I found myself smiling and whispering, "You're welcome, Camille."

One of her brothers once mentioned to me that when their dad died, they didn't feel like the funeral reflected who he really was, and they'd been disappointed. They wanted something better for Camille. All of Camille's brothers wanted to speak to Fr. Ron about their sister, sharing stories about her, and talking about who she really was. I knew how important this was to them, so I was glad he agreed to come to our home to meet with them.

It is beautiful how people come together to show support and love when someone loses a loved one. Camille's family was very appreciative of the kindness and love they were shown at that tragic time. Peter and I were so thankful for all of the support that our family and friends shared with us.

What really touched us was that members of our own parish were there to help us in our time of pain. Peter belongs to a Catholic organization in our parish: the Knights of Columbus. These men stepped up to help him. Even though the funeral wasn't at our parish, our priest, the altar server at the Mass, and the men who put on the reception were all Peter's fellow Knights.

It helped us realize how lucky we were, belonging to such a wonderful church community, and it reminded us of how important it is to be there for other people. At some point in our lives, we will all have to go through some type of painful journey. It makes life so much easier, knowing you are surrounded by people who care.

Death Is a Natural Process

The funeral was beautiful. Camille would have been proud. A few things happened that we laughed at later, and because they made us laugh, we swore Camille had been with us.

First of all, the Gospel reading Peter's mom had chosen was not the reading that ended up being used. We laughed, thinking Camille would surely want to have the last say in her funeral. She was very independent and would have wanted things said her own way.

Secondly, as the family lined up to greet the people, one of Camille's coworkers came up to Peter and asked if the mistake in the program was done on purpose. Peter didn't know what he was talking about, so the gentleman held out his copy of the program. He said one of the songs had been listed as, "Song of the Angles" not "Song of the Angels."

So many of the family members had read the program over before the funeral day, looking for errors, but not one of us had picked this little detail up. Camille, of course, was a carpenter, and she had a wonderful sense of humour. Thanks for the last laugh, Camille!

Rainbows

Every one of us is different. When we are faced with the death of a loved one, we don't know how we will react. Sometimes we are surprised by the way we or other people cope.

Often we discover someone we know has an addiction or another major issue, though the cause may take years to appear. Sometimes the reason for their addiction or other issue is revealed as coming from a loss that was never properly dealt with. When I realized the feelings I'd kept hidden were beginning to surface, I understood why I was becoming more emotional. Once I gave myself permission to remember all those difficult times from years before, I began to write. It seemed that once I started writing, I couldn't stop.

Reliving all that pain was both difficult and painful. I found comfort in realizing I was bringing it to the surface and dealing with it. I began to remember all kinds of things I had forgotten or hidden away. Lots of times the memories were so painful that I couldn't help crying. Some days I reread what I had written and wondered how I had gotten through it all.

People used to say I was a very strong person, but I'd never thought so. I thought I was probably just trying to survive. As I looked back on my writing, I realized they were right. I was strong. I just didn't see it in myself.

My Mary

The beautiful thing about life is that anything is possible. What I found amazing is that when I began to heal, something beautiful happened to me.

I am the type of person who doesn't see life as black and white. As I'm writing this section, I bring out a quote book one of my daughters once gave me. She knew I loved reading quotes and thought I could use this book to write down any I came across that touched my heart. I added my own quote to this book, and it's the only quote I've ever made up. Sometimes I'm having a conversation with someone and what I hear them say is either black or white. That's where I got the inspiration for my own quote:

> *When you look at things in life as black and white, don't forget the rainbows. It is in the rainbows that you can feel such an intense love in your heart, a love that you know can only be the presence of God.*

I am so happy I choose to see the rainbows in my life. My wish for others is that they trust enough to allow themselves to see those rainbows. What had happened to me that was so beautiful? I think it was at the time that the three people I had loved and lost made a connection with me, right at the time I was trying to relive my past.

It was our twenty-fifth wedding anniversary. Our friends and family were throwing a party to celebrate this occasion, and in walked one of my cousins. She handed me a package, and when I opened it I discovered it was a necklace which she said had belonged to my mom. It had been out of my family for over thirty years. Her mom was getting ready to move, and she was sorting through some of her things when she came across my mom's necklace. When I think back, I can't remember my mom ever wearing jewellery. I'd even thought she might have been allergic to it. But I came to learn that she used to love wearing it years earlier.

Only a few people knew that I was in the process of writing, trying to heal those wounds from my earlier years. For this woman to walk in the door with a piece of my mom's jewellery from thirty years before was a shock to me. I thanked her but couldn't pay much attention to it at the time because of all the excitement of people helping us celebrate this marital milestone. I placed the necklace in my bedroom drawer, planning to take it out the next day, when I had more time to look at it.

The next day, still in shock, I took a better look. Having this treasure in my possession after so many years was almost unbelievable. I've placed the necklace next to me while I'm writing about Mom, because I want to feel close to her while I write this part. It is a beautiful, heart-shaped necklace with six pearls and a dark sapphire in the middle. The light is shining on the necklace, and for the first time I notice the dark sapphire is purple. Both Mom and I were born in February, and purple is the colour of our birthstone.

When I was given this necklace, I knew it needed work. The chain had been broken and its finish was dull because it had been put away for so long. I decided to take it to the jewellers. They had to send the necklace away, so I knew it would be a while before I got it back.

About a month later, I was sitting on the back deck with Peter, talking about Mom. The jeweller had called a few days before, saying the necklace was ready. I told Peter I was going to pick it up and hopped in the car.

When my mom died, I only kept two things that had belonged to her. One was a green sweater she used to wear. The other was the little statue of our Blessed Mother I had given her after she'd gotten sick. The sweater still hangs in my closet after twenty-seven years. Once in a while I'll put it on for a few minutes, just to feel close to her. Now I have the necklace as well.

My Mary

As I drove to the jeweller, thinking about my mom, I was still in disbelief that the necklace had come into my possession after so many years. I hoped they would be able to do a good job restoring it, but when I told the saleslady I was there to pick up my necklace, I was feeling a bit anxious, wondering how it turned out. This was one of many times in my life that I sent up a little silent prayer.

"Please Lord. Let them restore my mom's necklace so I can wear it."

The saleslady came back to the counter and slid the necklace out of the package, letting it spill out on to a velvet cloth. It shone, looking absolutely beautiful. The saleslady even commented on how beautiful it was. I tried to keep my composure as I thanked her.

"This is the best gift I could ever be given," I said, feeling tears well up in my eyes.

Walking out of that jewellery store and holding on to my mom's necklace that day, I was overwhelmed with emotion. I could actually feel my mom's presence through the chain, hear her say, "I'm sending you a piece of my heart, Patsy. I'm so sorry for hurting you."

I tried to calm down because I needed to drive home, but I couldn't stop the tears. I cried all the way home. When I came in the door, Peter could tell I had been crying.

"Are you all right?" he asked, concerned.

I nodded. "It's just that I feel my mom so close to me right now," I told him, and cried some more.

In my earlier years, I had wanted more than anything for her to apologize, to say she was sorry for giving me the responsibilities of an adult, when I only wanted to be a kid, like all my friends. I'd wanted to have a carefree life, not one filled with worries about running a household.

One time, when I'd visited Mom in the hospital, she stated that she knew I hadn't had an easy life. I'd held my breath, waiting for her to say, "I'm sorry. I should have been the mom, and you should have been the child." But those words never came.

I needed very badly to hear those words. I'd never told her how I felt about this, but that was because I believe it doesn't mean as much if you have to tell someone that you need to hear an apology from them. I wanted her to find those words in her own heart, without my prompting.

I guess what's so beautiful about love and life is that when we least expect it, wonderful things can happen, though we may not understand them at the time. Wonderful things, like making a connection with my mom, twenty-three years after she'd passed. This connection gave me such peace and comfort that it played a big part in my healing. I finally understood that she loved me, and she was sorry. Not even death could keep her from reaching out to me when I needed a mom the most.

When I started my journaling, I thought I might someday want to publish my writing, hoping it might help other people who were grieving. It might even help people who had buried their pain like I had. I eventually realized that writing was for my own healing. I did give it a title, though, just in case I did end up publishing it. The title was "Remembering That Only Love Is Real." After I finished writing about all those memories, what I concluded was that the most important thing in our lives is love.

I also realized that no matter how hard my life might have been at times, I was still blessed. I had loved, and I was loved. I turned out to be the person I am today because of all of my life experiences. I also learned that we can make a difference in people's lives just by reaching out to them. I am so grateful that God put people in my path along the way, people who helped guide me as I went through all of life's ups and downs.

The night my mom's necklace showed up in my life, I felt Nan reaching out to me. When my cousin John walked into our twenty-fifth anniversary celebration, he carried two gifts with him and passed one to me.

"This is for you and Peter," he said. "The other one is a gift just for you."

I was surprised and touched that he'd bought a gift for me, and I was very curious. When I'd opened the wrapping paper, I peeked inside the box and was met by the most beautiful pair of eyes. It was a photograph of Nan, framed for me by John. On the other side, he'd put a picture of my granddad. I had never met my granddad before, but I studied his picture, admiring how handsome he was in his army uniform.

I was so touched when I saw this picture. I couldn't believe that on the night of such an important milestone in my life, not only had Mom touched my heart, but now Nan seemed to be a part of it as well. Both of them had let me know that they were with me and were a part of this special occasion. I even saw the humour in my Nan's showing up, since, as I said earlier, I believed she picked my husband out for me after she died. You can be sure that twenty-five years after our wedding, she wasn't going to miss out on the party! I could almost hear her sweet, gentle voice, whispering, "I did good, dear."

Three months after our twenty-fifth anniversary celebration, Amanda, my daughter, was graduating from high school. When we began looking at the different scholarships being offered to students, one in particular caught my eye. The scholarship was for students with a parent or grandparent who had served in the war. When I saw this, I thought of my dad. He had served in the Second World War. I wondered, though, if she really had a chance of winning this scholarship, since my dad had been deceased for thirty-five years by then. Regardless, I had a strong gut feeling that she should apply.

A representative of the Legion called a few days later, and he told me Amanda had been selected for the $1,500 bursary because

Rainbows

of my dad's participation in the war. I was so happy it brought tears to my eyes. It wasn't so much because of the money. I was more pleased with the fact that my daughter would be getting a bursary because of my dad, a man who had not been in my life since I was thirteen. I was so proud. On that day, for the first time since he'd died, I felt him close to me.

On the day of her graduation, when they called Amanda's name, two uniformed representatives from the Legion, a husband and wife, presented her with the scholarship. My dad's presence was so strong that day that my heart was filled with joy.

The three people I had lost, and who I had loved so much, all made a connection with me over the painful months while I'd been working on healing the wounds in my heart. After all those years, they were with me once again. Sometimes it's easier to see things in black and white, but I was so grateful that I had chosen to look at life through rainbows. Rainbows are always there, but sometimes we need to look a little harder to see them. Look at the beautiful gifts I would have missed out on if I hadn't opened my eyes.

Building the Rosary Garden

(June 23, 2007)

From the moment David and DeeDee arrived home from Florida, plans for the Rosary Garden never stopped.

This would be a major undertaking. Next to the church stood a large statue of Christ the King, and the O'Neils decided they wanted the Rosary Garden to be built around this statue. They also wanted the cement stones that represented the rosary beads to be large enough that people could stand, or even walk on the stones as they said the Rosary. To make the garden even more inviting, they decided to put benches in it. DeeDee even signed up to take a gardening course. She wanted to make sure the right plants were planted in this very special garden.

As the plans for the garden took shape, the family discovered just how generous people could be. When Adam had been alive, their family and friends had decided to raise money for his trip to New York for treatment. No one had expected him to lose his life so suddenly because of complications from a blood clot. They had just finished raising the money by having an auction, and some of them had written cheques for Adam's trip. DeeDee called all the people who had given money and told them she would be happy to give them back their money. But every person to whom she spoke told her to use the money to create a memory of their son in whatever form they decided was fitting. When the time came to put the Garden in, the money went towards it.

My Mary

So many people worked hard, helping however they could, wanting to make this a reality for the family. Everyone seemed to want to be a part of the process of building a place to honour Adam and his love for the Blessed Mother. Construction companies, brick companies, nursery gardens, and many others went out of their way to help.

It was wonderful to witness how kind people can be. We got to experience firsthand how people can come together to offer support in a time of need. People understood how important this was for Adam's parents, and for his brother, Cameron. They wanted to make sure Adam would always be remembered. When someone dies, most people stop talking about them, often because they fear they will hurt the people left behind. In reality, what seems to hurt the most is when the person trying to cope with this loss feels their loved one has been forgotten.

The date was set for the Rosary Garden to be put on the grounds of St. Vincent de Paul Parish, the church Adam's family attended. The event would be on June 22nd and 23rd, rain or shine, and invitations were sent to everyone the O'Neils thought might want to take part. At least a hundred people showed up on early that morning.

DeeDee's three sisters were among the crowd. The sisters had lost their mom and dad at an early age, and they shared a beautiful bond between them. When anything went wrong for any one of them, all four came together. The men these girls had married were also close, and I was sure that when they all got married, their husbands knew in advance they would be marrying the whole family. How fortunate they all were, to have such a wonderful relationship. How lucky their children were, to see firsthand how important family is.

People came with shovels, wheelbarrows, and anything else they thought could be used in creating this loving project. The

Building the Rosary Garden

family's friends and family members came not only from the O'Neil's community, but from David's and DeeDee's hometown in Cape Breton. Adam had spent many of his growing up years there, and it seemed only fitting that the Cape Breton branch of the family would be part of it. They even had a family member come from as far away as Alberta.

Peter and I felt blessed when we were asked to be a part of this. From the time we landed on the grounds of St. Vincent de Paul Parish that morning, the feeling in the atmosphere was amazing. It was wonderful to be among all those people who wanted to show love, support, and understanding to the family. This was such a gift for those of us who took part.

Building of the Rosary Garden, St. Vincent de Paul Parish, Dartmouth, Nova Scotia, June 2007

My Mary

There was something magical in the air that morning, and I know I wasn't the only one who felt it. I realize now it was the Holy Spirit. Sometimes, when we are given the opportunity to work together and help each other, we are given a glimpse of how beautiful life can be, and how beautiful it is meant to be. When we work together with love, it's like we become one.

With every successful project, a team leader is needed. Marco, who had grown up next to the O'Neils, and who was more like family than simply a neighbour, was asked to head up the project. As we all came together that morning, we gathered around Marco, looking for guidance. We were eager to start.

We listened intently as he explained how all this would work, putting everything together so it would end up being a beautiful garden. It quickly became clear to us that we were being guided not just by a leader, but by someone who had loved Adam. We knew it was important to Marco that everything went well. He was playing a big role in helping the O'Neils as they gave a last gift to their son.

Before we knew it, we were all digging in. To people watching, I'm sure it looked as if we knew exactly what we were doing. By lunchtime of that first day, we could actually see for ourselves how it could all come together successfully.

The project began Saturday morning. By early evening, when we were leaving the grounds, we felt pleased that we had accomplished so much. We were a bit concerned though, because we wanted to finish most of the work on the weekend and the forecast for the next day was rain. The family told us that if it did rain the next day, they certainly didn't expect us to work in it. We could finish the following weekend instead.

But seeing the garden start to come together filled all the workers with such excitement. We couldn't imagine not finishing what we'd started.

Building the Rosary Garden

"No way!" we told them. "We'll put on our rain gear and keep working."

I think the moment that touched most of us the deepest was when the large concrete cross went up at the entrance to the Rosary Garden. It was a powerful moment.

Completed Rosary Garden

When Adam had first been diagnosed with cancer in 2002, David and DeeDee got in touch with their parish, asking for prayers for their son. Their parish priest, Fr. Pat, asked the family if they would like the Associate Pastor, Fr. Mark, to get in touch with Adam so he could spend time with him, and they could pray together. They thought that was a great idea, and out of this came a relationship Adam came to value.

From what I understand, the first funeral that Fr. Mark performed happened to be Adam's. After the cross went up in the Rosary Garden that morning, the garden needed to be given a special blessing. Even though this gentleman, who was now a priest, had moved on to a new parish, he was at the parish that day, and he ended up being the priest who blessed the Rosary Garden. The blessing he gave was so beautiful. There wasn't a dry eye in the place.

The Rosary meditates on the life of Jesus Christ according to Divine Revelation, and Fr. Mark talked about Adam's life by using the different meditations. We cleaned up after the garden had been put in place, and talked amongst each other as we worked. We all felt blessed to have been a part of this act of love. Being involved had been a beautiful gift for every one of us. Over those two days we got to experience how important it is be there for each other, and we were reminded that nothing is more important than love. We left the church grounds that day, feeling we'd been part of something beautiful.

What Is Your Calling?

How many times have people asked you, "How did you know what your calling was?" Perhaps they say they don't know what their calling is, and they don't know if they'll ever figure it out. I believe every one of us is given gifts, including messages that help us find our calling; however, sometimes we're so busy with life we don't hear those little whispers.

As I look back, I can tell you my whole life was spent preparing for what Jesus would someday ask me to do, though I didn't actually realize at the time that comforting people was my calling. I have always comforted people. Even before my dad died, I remember trying to make people feel better. I have always cared about people and their feelings, and because they sensed this, they often told me things they wouldn't necessarily share with others.

Sometimes, after I'd had a conversation with someone in pain, they would say, "Patsy, I can't believe I just told you that. I've never shared that with anyone before."

I would just smile.

I was blessed with two daughters, Melissa and Amanda, whom I love so much. The most important thing in the world to me was being a good mom to them. I wanted to give them all the love and support that each child deserves. I wanted them to have a childhood and the ability to be a kid. It was important to both Peter and I as parents that our children always knew they had a soft place to fall.

My Mary

No matter how many times I sat in church having a chat with God, I couldn't hear Him in the way I thought I should. I told Him I was ready to do His work and that I needed Him to please show me what He wanted me to do, but I never received a message. I knew He would let me know in His own way, when He decided it was time. He would know when my heart was ready, then He could call me to go deeper into my faith to do His work. But it was frustrating, not getting answers.

Now I understand that's because I was already doing exactly what He needed me to be doing at that time: being the best mom I could be.

So it wasn't a surprise that it wasn't until my youngest daughter, Amanda, was going away to university that I started realizing what my gifts were, and how I was going to use them.

I constantly use my gifts in my everyday life, spending a great deal of my time comforting people. The spring before Amanda started university, I started giving thought to what types of things I would like to do to help others. Both our girls would be on their own in the fall, and that would give me an opportunity to put some time into expressing who I was as a person, not just as a mom or a wife. This was the time for me to begin to really use any gifts I'd been given.

When God gives us gifts, He doesn't want us to keep them wrapped up with a pretty bow. He gives them to us so that we can share them with others. I guess this is where free will comes into our lives. We can keep these gifts wrapped up, or we can open and share them. It's our choice. God hopes we will look deep into our hearts and share, but the decision is ours to make.

The thought of working with the dying kept coming to me. It felt right. One day I came across an advertisement for a three-day workshop for people who were working with the dying, or for those who were interested in doing this type of work. This

What Is Your Calling?

workshop would be put on in the spring, which was still a couple of months away. Without any hesitation, I filled out my form and put a cheque in the mail.

In the meantime, I spoke to Grace, a nurse with whom I had worked with in Pediatric Intensive Care Unit. A couple of years earlier I had told her I was interested in working with the dying. Now, Grace was the nurse specialist for Palliative Care in the children's hospital where I worked. She explained to me that most children die at home, not in a hospital setting.

They really didn't need volunteers to visit the dying children, but mentioned that they offered children's bereavement group sessions twice a year. These sessions helped children deal with the loss of a loved one. She thought I would be well-suited for that type of volunteer work. Now I had an idea of the direction in which I wanted to head with my volunteer work. I hoped I could work with bereaved children as well as with the dying.

In reality, though, things only work out when they are supposed to. One day I came home from work a couple of weeks after I'd applied for the Palliative Care Workshop, and a letter was waiting for me from the hospital. I was anxious to begin the workshop, since I knew I couldn't work with the dying until I had taken this course. With a smile, I opened the letter, thinking it would give me the details of the course. Instead, it said that by the time they'd received my application form and cheque, the course had already filled up. They were returning my cheque.

I couldn't believe it. Instead of mailing the application, I could easily have walked it over the first day they were accepting them, since I worked right next door to the hospital. I hadn't realized at the time how fast this program would fill up. A couple of days had made the difference. They told me they would be offering another course in the fall, if I was still interested in attending.

Because I now knew what I wanted to do, like most of us, I wanted it right then. What I had to learn and trust was that everything happens in God's time, not our own time. I understand that better today because of all the experiences I have had, but at that time I didn't understand.

Upset, I called my husband at work and told him I hadn't gotten in the course.

"Patsy," he said, "you, more than anyone, know that things will happen when they're supposed to."

I did know this, of course. I always say exactly that to people. But it's harder to accept when you're the one to whom it's happening. I knew I would have to wait until the fall so I could get into the palliative course I wanted. I decided to see if I could meet with the bereavement coordinator for the children's group, to find out if I might be able to come on board as a volunteer.

He agreed to meet me for lunch, and we had a great chat. I was getting the feeling, however, that things might not happen as easily as I'd hoped. He already had his volunteers, and I hadn't taken any courses to do this type of work. All I could offer was my own experience. Having lost a dad at a young age myself, I could relate to how these children felt. I also had a passion to do this type of work; that was obvious even to him. I told him I would keep in touch, because the next session for this group would be in the fall.

Every time I ran into him in the hallways at work, I reminded him not to forget me. I remember laughing to myself, thinking I might end up being his worst nightmare. But I really wanted this. I truly believed this was my calling. Knowing it is one thing, but convincing someone else is not always easy. I knew in my heart that if I was really meant to do this, it would all work out. I just needed to have patience, to wait for it to all unfold the way it was supposed to.

Fall arrived before I knew it. I promised to have my application in the first day they were accepting them, and I even called to make

What Is Your Calling?

sure when the registration was so I wouldn't miss it. The day the registration started, I wasn't taking any chances. I took my application and cheque, and walked it over to the office.

The lady smiled when I handed her the application. "Yours is the first application we've received," she said.

"I wasn't taking any chances," I replied with a chuckle.

As I walked out of the hospital that day, walking back to work, I was almost on a high, I was so happy. This may sound crazy, but I felt like Jesus had just given me a high five. I remember laughing to myself at the time, thinking I'd better not share that one with anyone!

When you open up and realize what your calling is, more opportunities seem to come your way. At the same time as this was going on, my former parish priest, Fr. Irek, had decided to bring a full day program to our parish for children who were experiencing a loss, helping them heal and giving them hope. This was known as a "Rainbows" program, and he'd implemented the program in one of his previous parishes out west. When I read about this in our parish bulletin, then heard him talk about how helpful it was for children who were experiencing a loss, I signed up to be a part of it. We were given a book to read and a guide to help us prepare to work with the children.

One part of the training was doing a self-reflection on your own loss. I remember listening to the facilitator and thinking that I wished they'd had programs like that when I'd lost my dad.

I got more out of the program than I had imagined. As I was taking this workshop, I was still working through my own grief. After a day of training, I realized there had been more for me to grieve beside the loss of my dad: I had never grieved the loss of my childhood. This was a "light bulb moment" for me. It was a gift, after all those years, for me to finally be able to shed tears over a lost childhood.

My Mary

After all my attempts to have the bereavement coordinator take me on as a volunteer, he finally agreed.

"What about the training?" I asked.

"We'll train you at the session," he replied.

I took the Rainbows workshop on a Saturday, and that Wednesday I started the Children's Bereavement Program. Things just seem to have a way of working out when you're on the right path.

Sadly, even though it was such a beautiful program, not even one parent signed their children up for it. Unfortunately, that's a very real problem. Parents' lives are too busy, and sometimes our children's lives are as well. I was disappointed parents hadn't realized what a gift they would be giving their children. Children who suffer a loss, whether it be from death, divorce, or something else, need to grieve. If they aren't given this opportunity, they may run into all kinds of trouble years down the road. I lived it, so I knew it. I wished I could scream at the top of my lungs, "Please give your children this gift!" But I wasn't ready. I was still working on my own healing.

I was one of the lucky ones; I was able to put my hurt into writing. But what about those who couldn't do that? Even though this program never took off in our parish, it was a great contributor to my own healing.

We never know the effect things will have on people. I'm sure some of the others who took the training thought it was a waste, since we didn't get to help even one child.

Actually, one child was helped. She just happened to have grown into a woman who finally gave herself permission to heal.

Sketch of Jesus

(November 2007)

I'm sure the image will be etched in my heart forever.

I had just come home from a course I'd been taking at one of our local parishes. It was a study series for Catholic women who wanted to learn more about their calling and the gift of their femininity. It also helped the participants develop a closer relationship to our Blessed Mother. The course was being taught through learning more about sacred scripture and our women saints. I had gotten a call from DeeDee the month before, and she'd told me she'd signed me up for the course. When she'd read the information on it, she thought it was something I would really enjoy.

My first question was, "How long will this course be?"

"Sixteen weeks," was her reply. "Every Saturday morning."

I work Monday through Friday. My first reaction was not to jump up and down with excitement. I liked not having commitments on Saturdays, and I'd never taken a course like this before. Then I thought more about it. I started thinking this might be a great way to start Saturday mornings. I called my friend Roseann, thinking she might also enjoy getting together with women, learning more about our Catholic faith.

Roseann, DeeDee, and I started this spiritual journey together. Over forty women would be participating in the course, which surprised me. My background had always been more reserved. Seeing all these women filled with excitement at the thought of showing their love for Jesus was new to me. I wouldn't say they were particularly charismatic, but they were so full of the Holy Spirit it was contagious.

We broke up into four groups to give us a better opportunity of getting to know each other over those sixteen weeks. I have to tell you, despite my slight anxiety, I loved it right from the beginning. I was at a place in my own spiritual growth where I had more of an open mind with regards to learning. My heart was ready to soak in whatever it could, so I could be closer to Jesus.

One day in particular stands out in my mind. We were going around the circle in our small group, discussing everyone's week. I was trying to pay attention to what everyone else was saying, but I couldn't seem to keep my mind off the spiritual journey I was on.

Have you ever had a moment in your life when you thought, "I'm exactly where I am meant to be at this time"? I knew in my heart that I was being called to go deeper into my faith. As we were sharing in our circle, I had an overwhelming feeling that I had responded just as God had wanted me to. Tears started flowing down my cheeks. When it was my turn to speak, everyone turned to me. They looked surprised to see me crying.

I guess I was having a moment of grace. They all listened as I shared with them how blessed I felt to have been led to learn more about my faith, to feel closer to our Blessed Mother, and to be doing it with a group of women who were just as eager as I.

This particular Saturday, probably a month and a half after the course had begun, I came home and found Peter waiting in the kitchen, having already made coffee and tea for us.

We sat down, and Peter passed me half of the paper. I was looking forward to reading it. I opened the paper and stared. Right in the centre of one of the pages was a black and white sketched picture of Jesus's face. The image was so clear. He had the crown of thorns on His head, and the sadness in His eyes almost tore my heart out.

Sketch of Jesus

Illustration done by Tammy Barbrick

I frowned, glancing at the top of the page. I'd thought I was reading the religious section, but the banner said it was the food section. I was confused. What was Jesus doing in the food section? I slid the paper over to Peter and pointed at the picture.

"What do you see there?" I asked.

"Parsley," he replied.

"Don't you see Jesus's face with the crown of thorns on His head?"

He frowned, looked back at the picture, then back at me. He shook his head. "You're pointing to parsley on top of a sandwich."

I looked at the picture again, and sure enough I saw the parsley. Jesus's face had disappeared. I brought the paper back and stared at it, thinking back to the morning's course. We hadn't spoken of Jesus's crucifixion, so I had no idea why it had been on my mind. For some reason, I was being trusted with this little peek into His agony. Not only was I shown the agony, but I was given an image of a sweet and loving act on the part of our Lord. The greatest act of love He could have shown us.

This was a gift, and I realized I could go to that place in my mind any time I might need comfort or strength. It reminded me that Jesus understood all the pain that each one of us has to go through. He is there for every one of us.

Did I mention that I'm married to a very practical man? Peter never again mentioned what had just taken place. I imagine it was probably hard for him to understand the things that were happening to me, but I knew that he loved me. He has always encouraged me to be who I really was.

Feast Day of the Lady of the Rosary

The Women of Grace course certainly helped me grow spiritually. Once I got a taste of how wonderful it felt to have a more open and close relationship with Jesus and our Blessed Mother, I wanted more. The other ladies in our group felt the same way.

It wasn't a surprise that at the end of this course, someone in our group suggested maybe getting together every six weeks at each other's homes. Doing that would enable us to keep learning in a warm and relaxing environment. It was important that we get together, even if it was only occasionally, so we could continue to grow. We enjoyed one another's company, and we also felt it was a safe place for us to talk to others about our beliefs, a place where we wouldn't be judged.

It was at one of these get-togethers that I was given information that shocked me. Later, when I really thought about it, I realized nothing was a coincidence. It confirmed for me how special Adam had been. It was a lovely day, and we were sitting in Marion's yard, enjoying the beautiful garden and our time together. DeeDee hadn't been able to get to this little gathering, because she was away for the weekend.

One of the ladies in our group, Corrine, was a wealth of information about her faith. She was always sharing things with the rest of us, things we hadn't already known. As we were chatting that day, someone asked where DeeDee was. I never shared the spiritual

My Mary

experiences I had with the ladies in this group, especially the one on the night Adam had died. Corrine made a comment that her daughter and DeeDee's son, Adam, shared the same birthday.

Corrine nodded when we all looked interested. "It's true. Their birthdays are on October 7th, which is the 'Feast Day of the Lady of the Rosary.'"

I don't think this statement had much of an impact on the others, but it did on me. I was shocked and wondered why DeeDee had never mentioned this to me. Her son had appeared to me the night he died, and he had such a love of our Blessed Mother that a beautiful Rosary Garden had been built in his memory. I couldn't believe I'd never known his birthday was the same day as this feast day. I couldn't seem to shake this feeling of disbelief.

When I got home that day, I left a message on DeeDee's phone for her to call me when she got in.

When she called me back, I asked, "Did you know that Adam's birthday is the same day as the Feast Day of the Lady of the Rosary?"

"I had no idea," she replied.

We chatted for a while longer, and both of us agreed what a beautiful thing this was. After we hung up, I started thinking about this spiritual connection I seemed to have with Adam. The only thing I knew for sure was that ever since that evening Adam had appeared to me with Jesus, I'd been right in thinking my life would never be the same.

I wanted to learn more out about this Feast Day of the Lady of the Rosary. I was intrigued that a four-year-old boy loved "his" Mary with such strength, and seemed to be so comfortable with it. It amazed me that his birthday had fallen on the same day as her Feast Day. I started to ask questions about this special day. The short version I was told was that in 1571 in the great battle of Lepanto, the Christians defeated the Muslims by praying the

Feast Day of the Lady of the Rosary

Rosary. Because of this victory, St. Pius V established October 7th as the Feast Day of the Most Holy Rosary. This victory was attributed to Mary's intercession.

I was beginning to see our Blessed Mother in a different light. To me, she had always been Jesus's mother. I had never really thought of her as being my mother, to whom I could go in times of trouble. I had always turned to Jesus.

Last year, when I attended a Catholic women's conference, the speaker gave a small talk on our Blessed Mother. She mentioned that sometimes, when people are not as close to the Blessed Mother as they can be, and don't feel that motherly bond with her, that person might not have a close relationship with their own mother. It could also be that something had been lacking in their relationship with their own mother. I remember sitting there, listening, my eyes filling with tears.

I loved my mother more than anything, and I had always tried to help her be happy. What I didn't realize was that it wasn't my responsibility. When you are put into a responsible role at an early age, you start to think you're responsible for everyone's happiness. Of course I now realize that each one of us is responsible for our own happiness

Maybe this was the reason I never looked to our Blessed Mother as my own mother. What a wonderful feeling, finally realizing that she is our mother as well as Jesus's. Now I knew in my heart that I could go to her at any time, and she would give me comfort, strength, or whatever else I might need.

When the speaker finished, we were all asked to come up and receive a medal of our Blessed Mother. As we were handed the medal, the person who passed it to us gave us a hug and said, "Behold your mother." What a beautiful moment that was for me, and such a powerful one. Everyone needs the love of a mother, but for different reasons, that isn't always possible.

My Mary

If you are one of those people in need of a mom, the Blessed Mother is waiting for you to come to her. Take a chance; she'll never disappoint you. When I speak with other ladies at similar conferences, we agree that we are blessed when people come forth and put the conferences on. So many blessings and healings seem to take place at the events. Not everyone who attends needs healing, but I think most of the ladies would agree that at the end of the weekend we walk away with a burning desire to do God's work.

At our house we never prayed the Rosary while I was growing up. I did see prayer beads, but we were never taught to say the Rosary as a family. Years ago, my cousin, Ann Marie, happened to stay with Peter and I for a couple of nights. She and I began to talk about our faith, and she told me she was in the Catholic Women's League in her parish.

The Catholic Women's League is a national organization rooted in gospel values. It calls its members to holiness through service to the people of God. She looked forward to getting together with the ladies once a week to pray the Rosary. I am now a member of the Catholic Women's League, but at that time I wasn't. I told her I thought that was wonderful, because she seemed to really enjoy it.

"I've never prayed the Rosary," I admitted.

Shortly after she returned to her home, I received an envelope in the mail from her. I opened it and discovered a little book on how to pray the Rosary. I was touched that she would do such a thoughtful thing for me. Praying the Rosary was important to her, and she wanted me enjoy spending time with Mary. I kept the book and looked at it from time to time. I tried to say the Rosary, but I guess I just wasn't ready.

She did exactly what Jesus would have wanted her to do. She planted the seed. In most cases, that's all we're supposed to do. In time, God will be the one to decide when it needs to blossom.

Feast Day of the Lady of the Rosary

I did eventually learn to pray the Rosary, and it has become very important to me.

As I write this book, a small statue of the Blessed Mother sits on my speaker. I glance up from my keyboard, and Mary is looking at me. I ask her to guide me in my writing, to help me bring people closer to her and her Son.

This year at my parish I helped facilitate the same Women of Grace program that I had taken a few years before. I wanted to give women the same opportunity I had been given a few years before, to grow more spiritually. This little statue was given to me as a thank you from one of the women who had taken this course. We never know how these little acts of kindness will end up having such an influence on us. I am reminded each time I look up and see her, how thankful and blessed I am that she is a part of my life.

Adoration

(May 20, 2008)

The Rosary Garden is available to whoever wants to spend time there, to be by themselves or with a group. DeeDee mentioned to me one day that we should get a group together so we could walk the garden while saying the Rosary. I thought this was a wonderful idea. Ella, one of the ladies who had been in the course, organized this for us.

Bringing people close to our Blessed Mother is very near and dear to her heart. Ella made up brochures to hand out that evening, Marion brought flowers, and someone else came with a guitar so we could sing. Others helped out in their own ways. When we were deciding who would do what to make this special, DeeDee decided I would be the one to read the meditations.

Ever since then, I have continued to read the meditations whenever we do the Rosary in the garden as a group. It seems I have been given that special job, and that means a lot to me. After we do the Rosary, we go into a quiet room for Adoration. To end the evening, we have tea and coffee, and DeeDee always brings a cake. She asked the girl at the bakery to ice the cake with a design of the Rosary. It adds a special touch to the evening.

I would like to explain my understanding of Adoration in the Catholic church. The first time I experienced Adoration was at a Catholic women's conference. I'd been Catholic all my life, but like a lot of Catholics, I hadn't experienced all there was to learn about our faith. I believe many Catholics reading this will understand what I mean. The more I was opened up to my faith, the more I realized I didn't know about it. I didn't find this discouraging though, because I believe we learn things when we're supposed to. I didn't know all the theology, and that was okay. What was more important to me was the relationship I had with Jesus. The rest would come in time.

The Catechism of the Catholic Church states:

The mode of Christ's presence under the Eucharistic species is unique. It raises the Eucharist above all the sacraments as "the perfection of the spiritual life and the end to which all sacraments tend." In the most blessed sacrament of the Eucharist "the body and blood, together with the soul and divinity, of our Lord Jesus Christ and, therefore, the whole Christ is truly, really, and substantially contained." "This presence is called 'real'—by which is not intended to exclude the other types of presence as if they could not be 'real' too, but because it is presence in the fullest sense: that is to say, it is a substantial presence by which Christ, God and man, makes himself wholly and entirely present."

Catechism of the Catholic Church
(paragraph 1374)

At the beginning of the exposition of the Blessed Sacrament, a priest or deacon removes the sacred host from the tabernacle and places it in the monstrance on the altar for adoration by the faithful. The "monstrance" is the vessel used in the church to display the sacred host. When a person attends Adoration, they are given an opportunity to spend quiet time with Jesus. Although they are with other people, it seems as if they are alone with Him. Soft music is sometimes played in the background, and candles are lit.

Adoration

DeeDee had made arrangements with Deacon Bernie at her parish, since we wanted to have Adoration after the Rosary was said that evening. The invitation to say the Rosary together was open to everyone. Music played in the garden just before we did the Rosary, and the beautiful sounds helped set the mood for the evening. Those who weren't familiar with doing the Rosary felt they were given a gift, a special opportunity to be closer to our Blessed Mother.

When we finished saying the Rosary, we went back inside the church and everyone found a place where they were comfortable. Music played softly, and all kinds of candles were lit. After a short time, Deacon Bernie entered with the consecrated host in the monstrance. Adoration is so peaceful; I don't think anyone could help but feel close to Jesus.

DeeDee and David didn't know that when we went into Adoration, the deacon had decided to begin by reading the eulogy from Adam's funeral. He wanted to do it that way so the people attending would really understand who Adam was. It was beautiful.

DeeDee and David then showed a DVD which included pictures of when we all worked together, building the Rosary Garden. The background music on the DVD was beautiful. We weren't surprised to learn the band was The Rankins, a family from Cape Breton. Cape Breton will always be home to the O'Neils no matter where they live. The song they had chosen for this was "Fare Thee Well." We were all so touched. I don't believe there was a dry eye in the place.

I had only attended one other Adoration before this, and it had been the month before, at a Catholic conference for women. When I saw the deacon go over to pick up the monstrance, I thought he would just be leaving the room afterward.

But there weren't as many people at this Adoration as there had been at the conference. Because of that, the deacon was able to go

My Mary

around the room and stand in front of each one of us, holding the monstrance.

When I looked over and saw him standing in front of the person closest to him, the only way I can describe how I felt was as if someone had just handed me a million dollars I hadn't known I'd be receiving. As soon as I realized he would be coming to stand in front of me also, tears began pouring down my face. I have no idea why, but what came to my mind was, "Father, have mercy on me." I kept saying that in my mind, and I felt so much peace in my heart by the time the deacon came to stand in front of me.

After it was all over, we left the room to have coffee and cake. One of the ladies with whom I had taken the Women of Grace course told me the deacon had asked her who I was.

"Why?" I asked.

"He said that when he got to you with the monstrance, he froze. He couldn't move when he tried to walk away. He tried to move a couple of times, but couldn't."

I had never before attended an Adoration when the priest or deacon had stood in front of me holding the monstrance, so I didn't realize he'd stayed in front of me longer than he had with the rest of the people in the room. Ella had been to many Adorations before this one, and she said she'd noticed.

I was having so many different spiritual experiences by this time that nothing really shocked me anymore. I wasn't sure why these things were happening to me, but I trusted God had a plan that included me. I tried not to put too much of my energy into wondering why or what it all meant. Of course I was curious, but I just tried to keep learning and growing in my faith.

One thought did cross my mind, though. Maybe this was a sign for David and DeeDee, showing them that I did have a real spiritual connection with their son, Adam. Maybe it confirmed

Adoration

that what I had told them in December 2005, about Adam and Jesus coming to me on the night he died, had been true.

I wanted to talk to the deacon, but I had a very short window of time in which to do that. Everyone had just finished cleaning up, and they were all getting ready to leave. I didn't want to ask people to wait for me while I talked; however, I knew that if I could ask the deacon just one question that had been burning in my heart for a long time, I would be happy with that for now. I wanted to share with him what had happened the night Adam died, but I knew that would have to be at another time.

I asked him if I could please speak to him for a few minutes, and he agreed.

"Deacon Bernie," I said. "I have been having many unusual spiritual experiences, and I know in my heart I am being called by God." He nodded, focused on what I was saying. "Sometimes these experiences are very difficult for me. What I want to know is if it is always so painful when these things happen to people."

He explained to me that each one of us has different experiences when it comes to our faith. God reaches out to us in many different ways, and yes, it can be painful for some.

When DeeDee and I drove home that night, I told her I would like to have a conversation with Deacon Bernie sometime about Adam. He'd known Adam, and I wanted to find out what he thought of the experience I'd had the night Adam died.

Like everything else, things happen when they are supposed to. A week before this book was going out to be edited, I called Deacon Bernie. I felt it was important that he know that the experience he'd had at Adoration that night, standing in front of me with the monstrance, would be included in the book. When he and I spoke, I shared a lot of the experiences which had happened to me since the night Adam had died. Deacon Bernie is a very spiritual man. He understood that sometimes we simply don't know

My Mary

why things happen to us when it comes to our faith. We learn to trust and hope that, in time, things may be revealed.

I have been to other Adorations since then. What happened on that night—with the person holding the monstrance being unable to move when he got to me—has never happened again. It only happened during the Adoration when Adam's eulogy was read.

Palliative Care Volunteer

I was so happy when I finally got to attend the workshop for Palliative Care training. The first day I attended, I sat by a lady I had just met, and we were having small talk. She asked me where I was planning to do my volunteer work.

"I'm not really sure," I replied honestly.

I knew in my heart and soul that I was being called to this type of work. I also believed I would end up where I was supposed to. When one of the facilitators got up to speak, I noticed her name tag, and I recognized her name from a conversation I'd had with a gentleman with whom I'd done volunteer work in the Children's Bereavement Program.

The lady was Jim's supervisor from a local hospital, and she was in charge of the volunteers in the Palliative Care Program there. He'd told me he had spoken to her, and she unfortunately hadn't been taking on any more volunteers. After she finished her talk, I went up and introduced myself. We had a chat, and I told her of my desire to work with the dying. I said I knew she wasn't taking volunteers, but would she be willing to meet with me to talk further about palliative care.

The local hospital where she worked wasn't far from my home, and it would work out great for me if I could volunteer there. She agreed to take my name and address and send me an application. I was so grateful just for the opportunity to submit

My Mary

an application. Two weeks later she called and invited me to an interview.

The only formal training I had for palliative care was the three-day workshop I'd just taken. I did have lots of experience with death though, including my immediate family members, other relatives, friends, and coworkers. Through conversations over the years, I'd learned some people had very little or no experience with death. It seemed I had lots of connections to people who ended up dying. When I went for the interview, I spoke from my heart about my passion to work with the dying. It wasn't long into the interview before she gave me the thrilling news that I could be on her team.

She was the perfect supervisor for me. Her name was Angela, and I was not surprised to discover "Angel" was in her name. After being a part of her team for a short time, I discovered people often referred to her as an "earth angel." She volunteered her time so that this Palliative Care Program could be put in place.

Angela had great compassion for the dying and their families. What a blessing it was for me to learn from her. She made sure we understood how important it was to treat dying people with dignity. Even though she had a full time job as a Palliative Care Resource Nurse, she spent a lot of time setting up visits for us. It was important to her that the patients and families had the support they deserved and needed at this time.

She arranged for me to go with another volunteer to visit patients until I felt comfortable on my own. Jeannine was my buddy, and we connected immediately. Her love for this type of work was evident right from the beginning. It wasn't long before she told me she thought I was ready to fly on my own.

I got in the habit of praying before I left the volunteer office and went to visit the patients. I always asked God to please let the patients see Him through me, but in truth it was I who got to see

Him through them. It is a privilege to be able to sit with people who are dying, to be able to help them or their families in any way. It was a wonderful and rewarding experience. Every time I finished for the day and walked back to the volunteer office, I sent up a silent prayer.

"Thank you, Jesus, for allowing me this sacred privilege."

What I also loved was that when a person is dying and accepts that fact, they are authentic when they have a conversation. It really touched my heart, being able to have this type of conversation with someone, a real heart to heart talk between two souls. There is no room for ego when people are dying.

Sometimes people ask if I find palliative care work to be depressing. The truth is that I didn't. It's amazing to witness that sometimes more living goes on when people are dying. I was privileged to be able to see a lot of beautiful things.

Yes, it can be sad. Sometimes you have to work on not taking that sadness home with you. Like in any situation in life, I connected with some people on a deeper spiritual level. I'll never forget one of the patients. We got along well on the first visit, even though it was cut short because he received another visitor.

The next time I went to see him, he told me he'd felt a special connection with me the first time I'd walked into his room. I smiled and told him I'd felt the same way. We began to talk, and it wasn't long before he began asking me what I thought of the afterlife. Did I really believe there was a heaven? I shared my beliefs, and he smiled.

Almost in a whisper, he said, "Patsy, I believe you. I feel so much better now."

This was one of the deaths with which I had a particularly hard time. I always looked forward to our visits and enjoyed when he shared stories about his life with me, including his dreams and disappointments. He said that even though some people might look at his life and think it wasn't that great, he had no regrets.

My Mary

I remember that Saturday morning. I'd gone to the nursing station to check on the patients I would be visiting that day. When I said his name, they told me he had died the night before. Of course he was in palliative care, but I hadn't expected him to die that fast. Things can change very quickly when a person is terminally ill. I was very thankful that when I went to check on the other patients I had, they were asleep or already with a visitor.

When I walked into my house that day, Peter came to the door, concerned because I was home early. He could tell by looking at me that I was upset. Peter always understood how important this work was to me. He did whatever he could to support me. I told him one of the patients with whom I had really connected had passed away the night before.

"Are you okay?" he asked.

"Actually, I'm not," I said, tears rolling down my face.

He gave me a hug, then I went to our closet and put my sneakers on. "I need to walk," I told him.

This particular death hit me hard. The gentleman and I had enjoyed a conversation one day, during which he told me he wanted to share something with his family, something that he had never told them before. He wanted to wait until Christmas to tell them, but he'd shared the story with me during our conversation. A few weeks before, I had bought him a journal, and he was very grateful when I brought it in to him. Sometimes he shared with me what he'd written in it.

It's the little things in life that we do for others that mean so much.

I wondered if he'd ever had a chance to tell his family. I felt a strong need to be at this gentleman's wake. No matter how hard it might be, if he hadn't had the opportunity to share the story with them before he died, I knew I needed to do it for him. I did go to his wake, and when I spoke to his family I learned he'd never been able to tell them, so I did. They thanked me, and as I walked out of the funeral home that evening, I imagined him smiling down on me.

I shared all of this with my supervisor, Angela, telling her I'd felt a strong connection with the man. She understood why I had to go to his wake.

"You were his messenger, Patsy."

I smiled and thought what a privilege it was for me to sit with everyone I'd been graced to visit. I am so thankful. I have learned so much about living from people who were dying.

I did palliative care work for three years. The beautiful thing about taking time to spend with Jesus is that He will lead you where He wants you to go. You will learn from each opportunity you are given. His whispers have taken me more into the bereavement work, and I learn more every day. I'm thankful for every opportunity I receive to comfort God's people. Every day I pray that when He puts people in my path who need to be comforted, I do so with love so they may see Him in me.

The Messenger

(July 17, 2008)

I awoke in the middle of the night, feeling like I had pulled something in my chest. When I moved even the slightest bit, it hurt. I also found it a bit difficult to breathe. No matter how much I tried, I couldn't seem to get comfortable.

I woke Peter with my stirring. "Are you all right?"

"I'm not sure. I think I may have pulled something in my chest," I replied.

I got up to go to the washroom, wanting to see if I felt any better once I started to move around. By the time I reached the bathroom, my head felt light. The last thing I remember was calling out to Peter, saying I thought I was going to pass out.

When I opened my eyes, I lay at the bottom of our bed. Peter was on the phone, explaining to someone what had just taken place. I couldn't move. My body felt like it was a dead weight. My first thought was that I must have had a stroke. Sweat poured down my face.

I had fainted once before in my life, so I had something to which I could compare. This had not been like a faint at all.

I lay with my head turned towards my bedroom window, feeling surprisingly calm. I don't know how or why, but I knew that whatever was happening was being divinely guided. This was part of God's plan for me.

My Mary

More than fear, I felt disappointed. I thought about all the experiences I had been having and wondered if I'd only had them in order to prepare me for my own death. I wasn't too happy with God at that moment. This wasn't how I wanted to die. At the very least, I wanted to be able to say goodbye to my children. I'd never forgotten how painful it had been for me not being able to say goodbye to my own dad. That was the last thing I wanted my children to experience.

I know we're all different. I'm a very social person. I always knew I wanted to have family and friends around me when it was my time to cross over, and I was very disappointed it looked like I wouldn't have that.

Strangely, one of my daughters had been at our home while this had been going on. She's usually a light sleeper, but she didn't hear a thing. Peter had called out to her, wanting her to come help him, but she never heard him. She didn't even hear anything when the ambulance arrived and the two gentlemen came into the house to see me.

We thought perhaps she hadn't come upstairs because she didn't come home that evening. After I had been settled at the hospital, Peter called her to tell her where we were. She asked him what happened, and she wanted to know why he hadn't woken her. He explained that he had called out to her numerous times, and that when we left for the hospital her car hadn't been in the driveway. Based on that, he assumed she'd never come home after all.

She told Peter that when she was getting ready to leave her friend's house that night, an awful feeling had come over her. She felt as if something bad was going to happen and decided it would be safer if she didn't drive the car home. She took a taxi instead.

I wasn't in the hospital long before they took an x-ray of my chest. Once they finished, they rolled my stretcher outside the room where they'd taken the x-ray. It was very early in the morning,

The Messenger

and everything was quiet. There didn't seem to be a soul around. I lay on my stretcher, looking around the hallway while I waited to go to my room, and thought everything looked very white. I felt vulnerable and alone and was trying to get my head around what had just happened.

It had happened so fast. Just the night before, I'd been at the same hospital doing my palliative volunteer work. Now I was the one laying here, and I didn't have a clue what the outcome would be. I've heard patients tell me many times how they'd gone into Emergency, and the next thing they knew, they were in palliative care.

Life can be so strange. We should never take things for granted.

From the corner of my eye, I saw a man standing across the room on my left. He and I were the only two in the room. He wasn't looking at me, but a strong feeling came over me, and I was suddenly certain he would be coming over to speak to me. I didn't want him to. I didn't like the feeling of being helpless, lying on the stretcher.

"Please God," I prayed. "Don't let that man come over to me. I'm feeling too vulnerable."

I watched as he stood and paced, then stopped in front of a poster on the wall. He seemed to be reading, but in my mind I was thinking, He's not really reading that poster. He's slowly making his way over to me.

"Please God, let that man stay there."

He turned, then my heart sank as he walked towards me. He looked to be about my age. His arm was tied up in a bright, multi-coloured striped scarf. The scarf was beautiful, but I hadn't noticed it when I'd been watching him from across the room.

He never said hi, but started off as if we'd already been having a conversation. "I always wanted to be a grandfather," he said, his smile weary. "My daughter called me tonight and told me she is going to have twins in January."

"Congratulations. That's really nice," I said, then frowned. I don't know what made me ask my next question, but I blurted it out anyway. "Were you in a fight this evening?"

"Yes, I was," he said.

He wasn't bleeding, it's just that his arm was all tied up in the scarf. The scarf looked out of place, and even more so when I remembered this was July. I didn't understand. If the gentleman had been in a fight, what were the chances that someone would give him a winter scarf?

He looked at me and gave me a wide smile. "You're going to be all right," he declared.

"I hope so."

The porter arrived to take me back to my room in Emergency. As she wheeled me away, the gentleman said something else, but I couldn't make out what it was.

I asked the porter, "What did that gentleman say?"

She shrugged. "He said he just made sure of it."

I was wheeled into my room headfirst, and when I looked above the door I noticed I was in room number twelve.

I gasped. "Oh my God."

A couple of days earlier, I had received an email about the number twelve and its significance in Christianity. It explained how the number twelve is all things of faith or of the church. I clearly remembered that email message and imagined it now.

Examples in the Bible of the Significance of the Number 12

All these are the twelve tribes of Israel, and this is what their father said to them when he blessed them, blessing each one of them with a suitable blessing (Genesis 49:28).

The Messenger

Do you think that I cannot appeal to my Father, and he will at once send me more than twelve legions of angels? (Matthew 26:53).

And when he was twelve years old, they went up as usual for the festival (Luke 2:42).

A great portent appeared in heaven: a women clothed with the sun, with the moon under her feet, and on her head a crown of twelve stars (Revelation 12:1).

Then Jesus summoned his twelve disciples and gave them authority over unclean spirits, to cast them out, and to cure every disease and every sickness (Matthew 10:1).

I couldn't believe this. Peter was waiting for me, looking concerned. As soon as the porter left, I told Peter I was going to be okay.

"Is that what they told you after they looked at your x-ray?" he asked.

"No," I replied, smiling. "A man came over to me while I waiting for them to read my x-ray. He told me."

Peter, of course, was confused. "Who was the man?"

"I have no idea," I replied. "A stranger."

Then I pointed to the number above the door, and told him about the email I'd received a few days before, talking about the number twelve. He still looked confused. How could I explain to him what I didn't understand myself? All I understood was that I needed to spend more time in prayer. I needed to quiet my mind. If Jesus was trying to speak to me, this was the only way I would hear Him.

When we got home from the hospital, it was a beautiful day, so we decided to sit out on our back deck. Peter told me he was invited to a function that evening, but didn't think he should go.

My Mary

I told him he should go, assuring him I would be fine. He shook his head, saying he wouldn't leave me alone.

"I don't think you understand," he said, sounding exasperated. "I don't think I'll ever get over what I witnessed."

"I passed out," I said, shrugging. "Lots of people pass out."

"No, Patsy. You didn't pass out. You checked out of your body."

Hearing my practical husband say something like that shook me up.

The next day I was speaking to one of my friends. I laughed and said, "Peter thinks I checked out of my body."

"Maybe you did, Patsy. Maybe something was printed on your heart," she suggested.

I had no idea. We didn't talk much about this after it happened. It was just another experience that I didn't understand. All of us have different experiences. They happen to us every day. At the time I don't think we're supposed to understand. God has a plan for each of us, so what we have to do is to learn to trust Him. Understanding why isn't important. He knows the plan, and as long as we believe He is leading us, we will be okay. A couple of years after this happened to me, Peter and I were sitting on the couch, enjoying a glass of wine after dinner, and the topic of the night I'd passed out came up.

"I thought I'd lost you," he said. "I know you went somewhere. I was just so relieved when you came back."

"Peter," I said, "if you ever told that to anyone else, they'd think you were crazy."

"I don't care," he replied. "I witnessed it, and nobody can tell me any different."

In the hospital where I work, there is a chapel. Beginning the January before this happened, I had started to go occasionally to the Mass they offered one day a week. That was the only time I spent any time there. I began to realize that when you become

The Messenger

closer to Jesus, He will always put opportunities or people in your path that will bring you even closer. When you spend more time in quiet prayer and begin to feel a loving bond with Him, you will want and need more time with Him.

In the hospital was a chapel where I could have gone five days a week, but I never took advantage of it. After this episode, I began spending a little time there every day that I worked.

The most beautiful thing about the chapel is the tabernacle. The tabernacle is a fixed, locked box, normally made of metal, stone, or wood, in which the consecrated Eucharist is stored. This means that Christ is truly present in the tabernacle.

A beautiful gift had been right in front of me all the years I'd worked there.

I don't waste time worrying about why it took me so long to realize this, because I now understand that only when our heart is truly open and ready will we be able to receive the gifts Jesus so generously wants us to have. Spending quiet time and sitting in front of the tabernacle helps me focus on Jesus. When everything around me seems to be in turmoil, I can keep my eyes on Him. It helps me hear those whispers clearer, when I might have second guessed them in the past.

Healing

(July 27, 2008)

It is a rare thing when a dream is filled with such peace that you imagine it must be close to what you'd feel when you're in God's presence. I had such a dream.

Peter and I had gone to Cape Breton the night before and were sharing a cottage with my best friend, Glenna, and her husband, Ronnie. We had a wonderful day together, and in the evening we sat outside enjoying each other's company, as well as the peace and quiet that comes with being in the country.

I don't always remember my dreams, but in the morning when I awoke, I could remember every detail of what I had dreamt the night before. In the dream, I had been sitting on a shore. To my right stood all kinds of mountains. In front of me was the ocean. In my dream I sat alone, enjoying the beautiful day. I turned my head to the right and looked towards the mountains, noticing a black lady who was flying very slowly towards me. She landed at my right side and sat next to me on the ground. I told her that the way she'd landed was a miracle. She agreed with me, then we both sat quietly, enjoying the beauty all around us.

We looked up towards the sky and watched the clouds. That was when I noticed that the first cloud that floated by was the outline of Jesus. It was amazing. The next cloud was in the shape of a cherub angel. The last was in the shape of an archangel.

My Mary

The dream felt so real. When I awoke, I couldn't believe the peace that filled every bit of my body. I never wanted it to stop, but knew that as soon as I got on with my life, I was going to lose that feeling. Glenna and I headed to the store early that morning. As we were driving, I told her about my dream, and the feeling of peace I had experienced afterward.

She had been having a few nightmares, so when she said, "You're dreaming of angels, and I'm dreaming of monsters," we both laughed.

Later that morning, Peter and I headed over to visit his mom, Irene, for the evening. As we headed down the stairs later, I passed by a table with a little angel sitting on it.

"Irene," I said, "That little angel reminds me of a dream I had last night."

I shared the dream with her, and she picked up the angel. "Well, you are meant to have that angel," she said, setting it in my hands.

"I don't want to take your angel," I replied, but she insisted, saying I was supposed to have it. It was a beautiful crystal angel whose hands were folded in prayer. I carefully wrapped her and placed her in my overnight bag, then brought her home with me the next day.

I enjoy all the angels I have at home, but this one felt a little more special in some way. She always reminded me of the beautiful dream that had given me so much peace.

The next summer we had a bereavement session at our parish for all the parishioners who had lost loved ones. I brought a few of the angels I had at home, wanting to set them on the table. I thought if there were angels on the table when people came up to light a candle for their loved one, it might somehow bring them comfort. I put a little wooden box on the table in which to place the candles, then set some of the angels next to the box. I put the

Healing

little crystal one in the front. As my parish priest, Fr. Ron, was walking by, he picked up the crystal angel and placed her in the centre of the wooden box, surrounded by the candles.

"That's a beautiful touch," I said.

As people came forward to light a candle for their loved ones that evening, she stood in the centre. The light from the lit candles shone on her, and I had to smile. This little angel was in the perfect place to bring comfort to people who were hurting. It reminded me of one of the Beatitudes:

Blessed are those who mourn, for they will be comforted (Matthew 5:4).

I sent up a silent prayer. "Please Father, help us bring comfort to the hearts who are here with us this evening and are hurting."

Earlier that day, I had found myself sitting in the chapel at the hospital where I worked. This would be the first session our parish would put on since the bereavement ministry first started. It was important to me that I be able to spend some quiet time in prayer before that evening.

When I had taken the Women of Grace course earlier, one of the main lessons we learned was about some of the women saints. The saint that touched my heart the most was St. Therese of Lisieux, who became known as "the Little Flower."

When I was growing up, my nan received mail every month. In it were articles from the Society of the Little Flower. I knew she loved this saint and thought maybe that was why St. Therese of Lisieux also became my favourite.

The humble sister had once vowed, "*My mission, to make God loved, will begin after my death. I will spend my heaven doing good on earth.*"

My desire was to help people while I was still down here on earth.

For a long time, I sent up a little prayer to her whenever I visited the chapel. "Please, St. Therese, say a prayer for me that I will do good on earth, like you want to do from heaven."

I was disappointed that I never had any idea if she heard me, and I told her that day. I guess I wanted some type of sign from her, just so I knew she heard me. I had heard that sometimes she would let you know she heard by showing you a rose or roses. On the evening of the session, one of my friends came in the door carrying flowers and a card. It was very busy, because people were beginning to show up for the session.

She passed me the flowers and the card. "I just wanted say thank you for the help you have given my family."

Her father had been quite ill, and I had done a few little things for the family. I was surprised to receive this gift. After I thanked her, I laid them on the counter, because I already had my hands full, trying to greet people as they were arriving.

At the end of the session, I threw everything in a bag. I placed the bouquet, all different kinds of beautiful yellow flowers, on top. It was a long evening, and I had to work the next day, so the only two things I took out of the bag when I got home were the flowers and the card that had come with them. Looking at them, I was reminded of how much it means to people when you reach out to them.

The next day, when I came home from work, I took everything else out of the bag. I was just folding the bag to put it away when something on the floor caught my eye. I bent down to see what it was, and stared with disbelief. It was a stamp with the picture of St. Therese on it.

I had asked for a sign. That sign had been shown to me in such a way that I couldn't doubt she had heard my prayers. I examined the flowers and, sure enough, there were a few roses in the bouquet. I got on the phone and called my friend, who had given me the flowers and card.

Healing

"Did you give me a stamp of St. Therese last evening?" I asked.

"Yes, after I had written the card to you I decided to put the St. Therese stamp on it," she replied.

I can't help it. No matter how many times I have these types of experiences, I'm still blown away by them. One thing I know for sure is that the more open I am to them, the more experiences I have. Some people would call them strange. To me, they are just a part of my life. They may be hard to explain, but I guess that's where faith comes into play.

I am still amazed by all the spiritual experiences I have had. I spend the time going over all that has taken place, knowing God has a plan for all of us. I believe eventually He'll give us a glimpse so that we may understand why we are given these different experiences. I don't think we'll ever really understand until we die, but I think He gives us little gifts of insight here and there.

The beautiful dream of the clouds and the feeling of peace that followed the next morning was one of those little gifts from Jesus.

Two and a half years after the dream, I was forced to lie very still as I recovered from eye surgery. It's difficult to stay motionless for so long, but doing that gave me time to think.

After all those years, I was finally healed. Grief is not easy work, but I had done what I needed to do so I could heal. Jesus was now ready for me to bring comfort to His people. He's the only one who really knows the wounds on our hearts. When we're ready, He will somehow show us what we need to do so we won't just bandage the wounds, but heal them completely.

Bereavement Work

Like with many people, there are lots of things in life of which I am unsure. Things I question and need to ponder.

One thing, though, was clear. I knew in my heart and soul exactly what Jesus was asking of me. He wanted me to comfort His people, and I knew He would show me how. I also knew that I did not want to disappoint Him.

I love being a volunteer doing bereavement work. Doing what I do brings me closer to Jesus. When I became involved in the children's bereavement groups, I knew this was exactly where I needed to be at the time. To watch the children's reactions, from the first day we met to the last, was truly a gift. For most children, these groups make a difference in their healing process. Among other things, it is helpful for them to understand that they are not alone in their sadness. It gives them an opportunity to meet other children who are also trying to cope with their loss and are trying to feel normal again.

When my dad died, I felt out of place with the other children for a long time. I remember the first day I went back to school after the funeral. I was still so upset, but it was important to me that I feel normal again. Most of the children stared at me before the school bell rang. I heard some of them whispering, asking the other children about the girl who had lost her dad. Some of them even pointed at me. It was a long, hard journey for me, and I had to figure out how to get through it on my own.

My Mary

I couldn't help thinking about my dad while I was sitting in class. One day, tears started running down my cheeks, and Sister McPhee came and led me out of the room. She and I walked around the school while she spoke to me in her gentle, motherly voice. I can't remember what she said to me, but I do know it helped. Sometimes we don't even realize that if we take the time to talk to the bereaved and listen to what they have to say, it can make such a difference in helping them get to a place in life where they can feel some type of normalcy again.

It seems to me that when you find out what your calling is, more opportunities come your way to use your gifts.

One day as I was attending Mass in my parish, an article in the bulletin caught my eye. Our parish priest, Fr. Ron, was hoping to start up a Bereavement Ministry if enough people were interested. Needless to say, I was drawn to join this type of ministry, a ministry in which I could use my own experience to help others who might be hurting.

Sometimes God will use you exactly where you are. Sometimes He'll send your opportunity right to your door. One day I was home from work, and the phone rang. It was a call from a service man. I had no interest in having anyone come over to my house that day to do any type of service work for us, and I told him that.

"It really won't take that long," he insisted.

I guess I must have heard one of those whispers, because I changed my mind and told him to come over. I showed him where to go and told him to call me if there was anything he needed. I made myself comfortable on our couch and began to read a book by Elisabeth Kubler-Ross, which I'd been given for my birthday. The book was on the five stages of grief. I had probably been reading for about twenty minutes, when he called out to me. I came to see what I could do for him, but he looked confused when I walked in.

"Oh, I thought you were in the room next door," he said, startled.

"No, that's my daughter in there," I replied.

I had met this gentleman the year before, when he'd come to our house to do service work. We'd chatted at that time, and I'd thought he was a very nice man. Sometimes when people need to talk they just need to hear a certain word before the floodgates open. Apparently, the word that was to start up this conversation was *daughter*.

"Do you also have a son?" he asked.

"No, I have two daughters."

He heaved a deep sigh. "I lost my son a couple of months ago," he said.

We began to talk. Before long he was sharing with me how hard it was to lose someone so young without any warning. He told me how painful it was not to be able to say goodbye to him. I knew that pain. No matter how you wish you had the chance to tell someone how much you love and would miss them, you're not always given that opportunity. It's a regret we carry in our hearts forever.

"Sir, I know this is hard to believe, but when you called out to me, I was reading a book on helping people with grief."

He began to cry softly. "I just don't understand why God would do this to a family," he said. As he was speaking, I heard a whisper in the back of my mind, saying, "Tell him about Adam."

That story isn't something I would share with just anyone, but I had a strong feeling that I was supposed to share it with this gentleman. I told him that we never understand why people are taken from us, and told him what I had experienced the night Adam died. I told him what Jesus had said to me.

"Maybe your son had important work to do for Jesus, like Adam did," I suggested.

I also told him about the Rosary Garden that had been made in memory of Adam. The gentleman told me he was Catholic, so

My Mary

I knew our Blessed Mother would have been a part of his religious upbringing. I thought he might find comfort in spending some time in the Rosary Garden. He and I probably talked for a half hour. As he was leaving, we hugged, and he thanked me. I've never seen him again, but it was a confirmation for me that Jesus will bring His people to you. Sometimes you don't even have to leave your home.

Because of my bereavement work, I had an opportunity to experience that. I had gone to a bereavement meeting for the children's group in March 2011. While I was there, I meet the lady who would be coordinating the children's group for the next session. I happened to meet up with her again that weekend at a friend's party. We laughed about how we'd just met that week and ended up at the same party a few days later.

Even though we hadn't spoken much, I knew how important bereavement work was to her. She told me she had lost her son in 2005. He had been ten years old at the time of his death. She was in the process of working towards opening a bereavement centre that would help not only children, but entire families who were grieving.

A couple of months later, I attended a Weekend of Grace conference. I sat with DeeDee's friend, Rae.

"I didn't know you knew Trish," Rae said to me.

"Trish?"

"The lady who is involved in the children's group," she said. "She told me she met you. Small world, I'm thinking."

"How do you know her?" I ask.

"I taught her son," she said. "He was the little boy who died at school just the month after Adam died."

I almost fell off my chair. The day I'd gone to tell DeeDee about what I had experienced the night Adam died, she'd told me about a dream she'd had of Adam carrying a little child. The next day she'd received a call from her friend, Rae, who was very upset.

Bereavement Work

Rae told her that a little boy she had taught the year before had passed away suddenly at school that day. Sometimes things come full circle in our lives.

"Oh my God!" I exclaimed. "I can't believe this. Rae, I might have mentioned to you that I'm writing a book. I started the book in February of 2011. I've already written about this woman's little boy in my book, months before I even met her or knew who she was. I can't believe Trish is the little boy's mom."

I tried to briefly explain to Rae what my book is about, then I told her about my experience the night Adam died. Rae is very close to his family, and I knew she'd find all of this hard to swallow.

"How could you have seen Jesus and Adam while you were driving?"

"I don't understand it myself. I just know that's what I experienced," I said.

We were both blown away. Rae was amazed with what I told her about the night Adam died, and I couldn't believe I'd met the mom of a little boy I'd written about in my book months earlier.

I looked across the table at Rae. "I may not have many friends left after all my experiences get out through my book," I say, laughing. Rae joins me in the laughter. "I may need you to be my friend."

In the fall, I was asked to do parents' bereavement sessions with Trish. This was a drop-in session, so we were never sure if we'd get any parents on a given night.

While I waited downstairs to see if any parents showed up, I had time to think. I realized I'd have to have a talk with Trish eventually and tell her that I wrote about her son in my book, months before I'd met her. I had no idea how this conversation would go. I didn't know her that well, and I wasn't sure how she might react when I told her. But one thing I did know was that it hadn't been a coincidence when I'd met her.

My Mary

No one showed up for that night's session, so I took advantage of my time alone with Trish. I asked her if we could stay a few minutes and talk before we left for the evening. I started off by telling her that I had always been a spiritual person, but I had recently become even more spiritual. I explained that I had experienced many different things I sometimes didn't understand, but that they had made my faith stronger than ever. Because of all these experiences, I now had a closer relationship to Jesus and our Blessed Mother.

Then I told her that I had written about her son in my book a few months before I'd met her. I knew she was surprised. How could she not be? I told her of a few of my experiences, then asked if I could have her permission to write about our crossing of paths. Even though she didn't understand how these things could happen, she was open to the fact that they did.

Her little boy's name was Alex, and the centre that Trish and her family were working on and hoping to open was called Alex's Safe Harbour. I was privileged once again when I saw the love that goes well beyond the death of a child. How beautiful to find comfort in knowing that with God, all things are possible. Who knows? Maybe someday I will be helping out with Alex's Safe Harbour. I only know that wherever I end up, God will be sending me there.

Divine Mercy

(April 18, 2009)

Before this particular Easter season, I really only heard about the Chaplet of Divine Mercy briefly when some women from the Women of Grace program I had taken came to one of our gatherings after the program, which happened to be at my house that particular day. This Chaplet, I learned, is a Roman Catholic devotion, based upon visions of Jesus by Saint Mary Faustina Kowalska in 1935. This Polish sister was canonized as a Catholic saint in 2000.

I was told that this particular saint said she received prayers through visions and conversations with Jesus. In return for the recitation of these prayers, specific promises would be made. It was also mentioned that if it is compatible with God's will, many things can be obtained with this prayer.

I attended the liturgical service that Good Friday. I had read in the church bulletin earlier that if anyone wanted to do the Divine Mercy Novena as a group, they could come to the parish that evening. I really didn't know a lot about this novena. I guess it goes to show that just because you're a particular religion doesn't mean you know everything about your faith. There is so much to learn.

When your heart is open and ready to learn more about your faith, those opportunities will come to you. Being more open to learning was the key to helping me to have a better perspective about my faith.

My Mary

This particular novena would begin on Good Friday. It is said for nine days, and this is where the term *novena* comes from. There would be certain prayers you would say on each day. Each of the nine days of the novena asks for God's mercy for a specific group of people.

The last day would be the most difficult intention of all, namely to pray for the lukewarm and indifferent. I started thinking about how much this must hurt Jesus—when people are aware that He does exist, but just can't be bothered to have Him in their lives.

Every time I leave my parish on Good Friday, I am always so thankful to be reminded of what Jesus did for us. Being able to relive His crucifixion and His death at Calvary helps us understand how much He loves us. We get so caught up in our everyday lives that sometimes we forget to thank Him. We take for granted what He did for us. That one specific day gives us an opportunity to remember again how He suffered for us.

This is also a day in our Catholic faith when we abstain from meat. Like many Catholics that day, my family was having seafood chowder instead of meat for dinner. Just as we were getting dinner ready, the phone rang. It was my friend Roseann.
"Are you going to church this evening to do the novena of Divine Mercy?" she asked.

"I thought about it, but no," I said. "I won't be attending. Dinner is just about ready." We chatted for a few minutes more, then hung up.

About ten minutes later, Peter was just pouring our chowder into our bowls when the phone rang again.

"Patsy, I'm sorry to be calling you again, but you simply have to do the novena tonight," she said, her voice sounding almost urgent.

"Roseann," I said, laughing. I knew the novena would be starting in about twenty minutes. "Peter is just putting the chowder in our bowls. We're just about to sit down."

Divine Mercy

"I'm not usually so bold," she said. "But I have a very strong feeling that you're supposed to do the novena this evening."

This kind of thing was very out of character for Roseann. Peter, who could hear the conversation taking place, started transferring the chowder from our bowls back into the pot.

"Go ahead," he said. "We can eat when you get back."

I rushed out the door to meet her so I wouldn't be late. As we walked into the parish, our priest was handing out information on the novena. Through the pamphlet, I learned that the novena required that I go to confession and receive the Eucharist on the Feast Day. I love receiving the Eucharist, but I wasn't jumping up and down for joy with the knowledge that I would have to confess my sins as part of doing this particular novena. Then again, I'd been trying to find comfort in getting back to going to confession, and I realized this opportunity would give me more practice, which was probably part of God's plan.

It was nice to say the novena with other people. Because of scheduling, I did it by myself for the rest of the week. On the ninth day, I was sitting upstairs on the couch, just finishing saying the novena, when my daughter Amanda called to me. She needed me to throw her down a box of Kleenex. I got up from the couch and gave her the box of Kleenex, then went to gather up my prayer beads and purse. As I was walking towards the couch, I saw something shiny where I'd been sitting. I knew it was a medal, but I didn't remember having one in my purse. I examined the medal and realized it was the Divine Mercy medal.

My first reaction was shock. I couldn't remember putting a medal in my purse, let alone a Divine Mercy medal. It seemed strange that on the last day of doing this novena, the Divine Mercy medal had shown up. It had come from my pouch, I realized, since I keep my prayer beads in my purse. Obviously when I went to get my prayer beads to do the novena, it had fallen out. I had been

My Mary

using those prayer beads for eight days before this. It was only on the last day, just as I finished the last prayer, that I discovered the medal, sitting right where I had been doing the novena.

I called Roseann to make arrangements to go to confession, because this was the last day of the novena. Doing the novena correctly meant I'd have to go to confession, and I hadn't gone yet. I told Roseann about finding the medal on the couch

"I'm not even sure where I got this medal," I said.

She reminded me of the day at my house months before, when the women from the course we had taken came over for a get-together. One of the women, Ella, brought information on the Divine Mercy novena and had given each of us a medal. I had put it in my pouch and completely forgotten about it.

If I had any questions about what Roseann had said to me about having a strong feeling I was supposed to do this novena, they were gone after I saw the medal on the couch.

Earlier that week, I had called the parish where we had decided to go for confession, wanting to make sure I knew the times for that particular day. When we arrived, we had to sit for a while, waiting for the priest to arrive. I started to wonder if maybe I'd messed up. That wouldn't be good. Then again, that's what I get for waiting for the last minute possible before arranging for this confession.

"Roseann, what if I got the time wrong, and we don't have a priest to hear our confession?"

"Well," she said with a shrug, "I guess we'll have to bring out the phone book and call a priest."

I chuckled, and we got up from the pew to go to the foyer of the church. Roseann spotted an old bulletin, and we looked on it for the times for confession. Sure enough, it was happening a half hour later than I had thought. I was relieved when I finally saw the priest walking towards the confessional box. I would have been disappointed if I hadn't done this part of the novena.

Divine Mercy

I understand why some people have anxiety when they go to confession. Some are comfortable, but I think a lot of us have a hard time with it. But the way you feel when you finish talking to the priest makes any anxiety you may have had worthwhile. We should take comfort in knowing what the Lord told Saint Faustina:

> *"When you approach the confessional, know this, that I Myself am waiting there for you. I am only hidden by the priest, but I Myself act in your soul. Here the misery of the soul meets the God of Mercy. Tell souls that from this fount of mercy, souls draw graces solely with the vessel of trust. If their trust is great, there is no limit to my generosity"* (1602, Diary of Saint Maria Faustina Kowalska).

On the way home, I asked Roseann if she would mind dropping me off at the hospital so I could do my palliative care volunteer work. It was supper time, unusually late for me to go to the hospital, and I was even later because I had mixed up the time for confession. But I figured it was better to go late than not go at all. I signed in and sent up some prayers before I went to visit my first patient, then I knocked gently on the door and entered the first room.

Two of the gentleman's family members were with him. His wife sat next to his bed, and his daughter sat in front of the window. I introduced myself, then asked how they were doing, and if there was anything I could do for them.

"Actually, I do have a question," his wife said.

I don't remember the question, but both his daughter and wife watched me intently as I answered. As I was speaking, the gentleman's son walked into the room. We were all introduced, and I went back to answering the question.

As I was finishing my sentence, the son glanced over at his dad and exclaimed, "He's not breathing!"

My Mary

It happened that fast. We buzzed the nurse to confirm that the gentleman had died. Every one of the family members was in shock. I stayed with them to try and console them. It was especially hard on them, because they hadn't expected it to happen as quickly as it had.

Afterward, I walked down the hallway of the hospital and realized this was the first death I'd witnessed since I'd started doing palliative care volunteering. I was at the hospital at a time I wasn't normally there, but I knew in my heart that I was there right when I should have been.

To be honest, I did feel bad. The family had been sitting by his side for days, waiting for him to take his last breath. When he finally did, they were looking at me and not at him. It was almost like he'd been waiting for me to come into the room, so he could take his last breath without his family witnessing it. This was one of those moments I had to trust that God had sent me exactly where He'd wanted me to be.

The next day was Sunday, so it gave me an opportunity to speak to my parish priest, Fr. Ron, about this experience. I felt better afterward, understanding that, when it comes to death, God would be the one to decide when we take our last breath.

I had often questioned the deaths in my own life. Why had I walked out of the room shortly before my nan took her last breath? Why, when I visited my dad for the last time in the hospital, did I not let him know how much I loved him?

I've heard many people agonize over their own experience when it came to their loved one dying, asking why they hadn't been present when their loved one had died. It wasn't as if they hadn't tried to be. They had left the room for just a moment and their loved one was gone. After this experience I realized that death will unfold as it's meant to unfold. The big challenge was trusting that only God knows when that time is right for us to join Him.

Foot of the Cross
(May 2009)

I read somewhere that when a soul is ready for a teacher, one will come into their life. I hadn't discussed the different spiritual experiences I was having with a lot of people, though once in a while I would share something in a conversation. A few close friends knew, but these types of things aren't something you normally go around talking about.

I certainly couldn't explain to people why I was having them, and I absolutely didn't want people to think I considered myself to be special just because these things were happening to me and not them. It was only that I was more open to the experiences. I also wanted very badly to do whatever work here on earth that God wanted me to do.

Now that I know I am getting closer to finishing this book, I feel more willing to share. I believe the time is right to do so.

One evening I was at a Pastoral Care meeting in our parish. As they do in a lot of meetings, sometimes conversations go off track and spark an entirely new discussion. That evening someone asked our priest, Fr. Ron, about his opinion on Purgatory. My perception of what he said was that everyone goes to Purgatory to be purified before they can go to Heaven.

I thought about this after I got home. I still couldn't wrap my head around the fact that the night Adam died, I had seen him with Jesus. If I had seen him with Jesus as soon as he'd died, then how could he have gone to Purgatory first? I was confused enough that I decided the time had finally come that I needed to share my experiences with someone who had training and experience in spirituality.

I sent an email to Fr. Ron, saying I needed to share with him that I'd had an experience in November 2005. It had told me something different from what I'd understood he was saying about Purgatory. I said I would like to have an opportunity to speak with him about this and other experiences I was having. He replied that there were many graces and spiritual favours extended by God to those dying, and to those who accompany them. Signs of consolation, hope and peace. This certainly helped clear up the confusion in my mind about Purgatory.

I made an appointment to speak to him later that week. When I arrived, he was still doing confessions, so I waited in his office for him to finish. As I waited, I was drawn to a picture on the wall. It was a beautiful picture of Jesus, standing behind his mother, His arms wrapped around her. What really stood out for me was that the Blessed Mother looked so normal, she could have been you or me in the picture.

I had never before seen a picture in which our Blessed Mother looked like this. To me, she always looked like a queen, dressed in a beautiful gown. This was the first time I had ever seen her look more like a mom than a queen, and this made a huge impression on me. I was becoming closer to our Blessed Mother all the time, and now I could actually visualize her in a regular mother's role, not just as Jesus's mother.

By the time Fr. Ron came to talk to me, I was so excited about this picture that I couldn't stop talking about it. I asked him if we could have our meeting in front of the tabernacle. I felt a very strong need to share all this with him while sitting in front of Jesus.

We sat, and I talked for almost two hours. It seemed once I started, I couldn't stop. He never once rushed me, and I certainly

Foot of the Cross

didn't feel I was being judged. Afterward, he read a passage from the Bible and explained to me that it is a privilege to be given such moments of grace, and that I must always remember to say thank you to Jesus for such a blessing. Because of these moments of grace, I now had a spiritual well from which I could draw. A well in my mind, to which I could go whenever I needed comfort, or whenever I needed help keeping my focus on Jesus.

As we were walking back to his office, Fr. Ron told me that if I ever needed protection, I should go to our Blessed Mother. Two years later I would remember this statement when I needed it the most.

I must have really been going over the top about the picture, because Fr. Ron eventually took it off the wall and told me I could borrow it for however long I needed it.

Just the day before, Peter had changed our bedroom around. I know this is difficult to believe, but a nail protruded just above our bed as if it was waiting for that picture. When I got home, I walked right into our bedroom and hung the picture there. As I lay in bed that night, thinking about the conversation that had taken place, I turned my face so I could look out the window. Even though the blinds were partially closed, light shone in from the streetlights and the moon.

I stared in disbelief, recognizing that as I was looking out the window, I was seeing a cross. The window has four panes divided by wood, but all I saw was the very definite image of a cross.

The curtain we have on our window is a single piece of cream cloth. It hangs over the window just as you would see a white cloth draped over a cross at Easter.

"What does it mean, the cloth draped over the cross?" I asked my cousin John one time.

"It means resurrection. Christ is risen, He is alive in our lives."

That same night I tried to sleep, but my mind was working overtime. I looked at the doors on my closet, and I saw a small cross and a large one. The doors have six panes: two smaller ones on top and four larger ones on the bottom. Before this moment, I had never actually identified crosses on my doors or on my window. Now that's all I can see when I look at them.

Ever since that evening, I see crosses everywhere. Obviously, they're not actual crosses, but I see crosses in so many things now. To explain what I mean even better, the next morning after I got up and was brushing my teeth, I looked down at the drain in my sink. I stared at the metal piece in my sink, that little thing that catches items if I accidentally drop them into the sink. To me, that little metal piece was in the shape of a cross. I have come to find great comfort in seeing these crosses.

Peter loves changing our rooms around. Probably a year and a half later, he wanted to change our bedroom around again. He had just started moving things, when I came into the room.

"What are you doing?" I asked.

"I'm putting the bed back under the window," he replied.

I hadn't shared with Peter that I was comforted by the cross I saw in the window when I lay in bed at night. I was hesitant to tell him.

"I like the bedroom like this. Can you please just leave it the way it is?" I asked.

"I really want to change it back," he said.

Maybe it was time to share with Peter the reason why I didn't want the bed put back under the window. I took a deep breath, then confessed. "I don't want you to move the bed from where it is because when I look at the window when I'm lying in bed at night, I see a cross. I find comfort in it."

He changed the room anyway, and I had to have a chat with myself. The house belonged to both of us. Marriage only works because people learn to give and take and respect their differences.

That night, Peter tapped me on my arm. "Look in the mirror," he whispered.

Foot of the Cross

The mirror was directly across from our bed. When I looked, I could see that the cross in the window was now above my head. I loved being able to still see the cross when I was lying in bed. All I had to do was look in the mirror. What was even more comforting for me now was that I was at the foot of the cross.

When Jesus saw his mother and the disciple whom he loved standing beside her, he said to his mother, "Woman, here is your son." Then he said to the disciple, "Here is your mother." And from that hour the disciple took her into his own home (John 19:26-27).

When you think about it, that is a beautiful place to be. What a wonderful gift Jesus gave us. As He hung from the cross, dying, He not only gave His mother to John, but to each and every one of us so she could be our mother also.

I loved seeing the picture of Jesus holding His mother every time I walked into our bedroom. I told DeeDee she would have to come over sometime to see it. One day she was dropping something off at my house and I told her to come up to see the picture in my bedroom.

She walked in the bedroom and looked at the picture. She gasped, then collapsed on my bed and began to cry.

"DeeDee, what is it?" I asked.

She told me that when she looked at the picture, she could see Adam holding her the same way Jesus was holding His mother.

"For a while now, I haven't felt Adam around me," she said. "When I look at this picture, I can imagine him holding me again."

I was so privileged to witness this deep love between a mother and her son.

"DeeDee, this picture was meant for you," I said. "It's a message from Adam. He knows how much you miss him, and he wants you to know he'll always be with you."

My Mary

I believed this picture had done what it was meant to do. It was time to return it to Fr. Ron. By taking the picture from his wall and lending it to me, Fr. Ron had no idea how much of an impact it would have on two women's lives: one woman who was trying to have a closer relationship with our Blessed Mother, and a mom who was trying not lose connection with her son. I ordered prints for myself, DeeDee, and Roseann, who had been with me from the beginning of this spiritual journey.

To me, the picture showed that the Blessed Mother wasn't just a queen, but a real mother. A mother to whom I could go any time I needed comfort or encouragement.

To DeeDee, the picture brought a sorely needed message from her son. I believe it helped her understand that even though Adam was no longer physically with her, he would always be close to her heart.

Walk with Jesus on the Beach

(June 2009)

Months before, DeeDee had invited a few friends over to her house for a Mexican dinner. The four of us, DeeDee, Roxy, Martha, and I made sure we got together at different times of the year, because we didn't want to lose touch with each other. Even though we all had busy lives and our own separate friends, whenever we crossed paths we felt drawn to maintain this friendship.

We bought season tickets to the Pop Culture at the Symphony, and we even tried to have a book club, but that just didn't work out. We spent more time laughing than talking about books. Maybe it had something to do with the name we chose for the group: the Chardonnay Book Club. We just couldn't seem to get serious about it, but we did enjoy telling people the name. It also became a tradition for the four of us to pick a date at Christmas and gather at my house for dinner where we exchanged little gifts with each other. We all looked forward to this.

Our husbands were invited to this particular dinner at DeeDee's. While we were enjoying our time together, David's brother, Tim, and his wife, Lois, came by for a visit.

As DeeDee was introducing us, Lois laughed. "So this is the Chardonnay Book Club I've heard so much about."

We had a wonderful evening. At the end of night as we were leaving, Lois said, "Why don't you girls plan a weekend and come over to Prince Edward Island?"

My Mary

DeeDee had already told us that Tim and Lois lived in a beautiful house on the beach. She enjoyed spending time there herself, and especially enjoyed their in-house theatre. We all thought this was a great idea, and promised to come visit Lois soon.

It didn't take us long to pick a date for our trip to Prince Edward Island. We decided June would be the month. DeeDee invited her neighbour, Maria, to come along with us, and we all piled into the car, happy to get away and spend some time with just the ladies. When we arrived at Lois's beautiful house, we were very excited. She treated us like royalty.

For probably a year before this getaway, I had done a specific meditation when I felt I needed to be close to Jesus. I was always on the beach with Him, and His long white robe just skimmed the tops of His bare feet. He and I walked the beach and talked. The meditation seemed so real when I was in it. I could even see my hair blowing in the wind.

Sometimes I smiled during this mediation. At other times we seemed to be in deep conversation. I never knew what He was saying, because He spoke not to my ears, but to my heart. I did have a sense, though, that whatever He was telling me was important. I almost felt as if He were trying to help me understand things. What things? I have no idea, but after this meditation I always felt comforted and close to Him.

Today was the last day before we left Prince Edward Island.. After breakfast we decided we would enjoy the theatre again. As we were all heading downstairs to watch a movie, I changed my mind. I decided I would take a shower before joining the other ladies.

It was a beautiful weekend, and I was reminded of how blessed I was to have these women in my life. We were all happy and content, but I think most of all we were thankful. After the shower, I came downstairs to join them and noticed Martha and Roxy weren't there.

Walk with Jesus on the Beach

"They decided to go for a walk on the beach," one of the women informed me.

"I think I'll go join them," I said. I'd take walking on a beach any day, over watching a movie.

As I was walking towards the water, I felt at peace and filled with contentment. I glanced up and down the beach, but couldn't see my friends. As I bent to take my shoes off, I noticed footprints in the sand. Of course I knew these weren't Jesus's footprints, but when I saw them, they reminded me of the poem, "Footprints in the Sand." I slowly stood and when I did, I knew Jesus was standing right in front of me. The wind was blowing, just like in my meditation, but this wasn't either a meditation or wishful thinking. I couldn't see Him with my eyes, but I knew in my heart that He was there with me.

I whispered very gently, "Jesus, You're here."

My heart filled with peace. He and I strolled down the beach, but when we came around the bend I still couldn't see my friends. A couple of times we stopped and looked out at the water. I knew He was telling me things in my heart.

How can our mind understand such things? I don't have a wild imagination, and I consider myself to be a well grounded person. My eyes filled with tears, and my heart with such love and gratitude that I was being given such privileges. I didn't think I deserved them. To be honest, it's not easy to have experiences like these. Sometimes I have to really talk to Jesus and pray about it. I pray I am strong enough to trust and believe, that even though I don't understand the things I have experienced, I know He does. I needed to search deep in my soul, and remember the trust between a child and a father.

My Mary

The Father and the Child

*The Father spoke:
Come, child, let us journey together.
Where shall we go, Father?
To a distant land, another kingdom.
So the journey will be long?
Yes, we must travel every day.
When will we reach our destination?
At the end of your days.
And who will accompany us?
Joy and Sorrow.
Must Sorrow travel with us?
Yes, she is necessary to keep you close to Me.
But I want only Joy.
It is only with Sorrow that you will know true Joy.
What must I bring?
A willing heart to follow Me.
What shall I do on the journey?
There is only one thing that you must do,
Stay close to Me. Let nothing distract you.
Always keep your eyes on Me.
And what will I see?
You will see My glory.
And what will I know?
You will know My heart.*

*The Father stretched out His hand.
The child, knowing the great love her Father had for her,
Placed her hand in His
And began her journey.*

(Cynthia Heald)

Walk with Jesus on the Beach

It seemed like a long time before I caught up with my friends. I never said anything to them about what I had experienced on the beach. Both ladies knew about the night Adam died, that I had seen him with Jesus, because shortly after I'd talked to DeeDee about it, we'd had our Christmas get together at my house, and DeeDee had asked me to tell them all what had happened that night. So I did. I don't think they were shocked, liked some people might have been.

Roxy's husband had passed away. One day, when she came over for one of our Christmas get togethers, she was a bit early, so we sat down to enjoy a glass of wine before the other ladies joined us. I told Roxy that I'd had a dream of her husband the night before. In the dream he had been in my basement. The basement was made of ice, and when I came down the stairs he sat in the middle of the room, on a little igloo. I already knew he had died, so I was shocked to see him in my dream. I asked him how he was, and he looked at me with such a beautiful smile on his face.

"I'm so happy Roxy and the girls are doing well," he said.

Then I woke up. I know telling Roxy about the dream gave her great comfort, but I was confused. I found it strange that the basement in which he sat was made of ice. Roxy told me that he hated winter. He had been a bus driver, so he had to be out driving in the bad winter weather all the time. I'd had no idea how much he hated the winter, but I guess this was a sign for her.

I know these are not things you can go around talking about all the time. Most people don't understand. Sometimes you just know when you are supposed to speak about it. Maybe at those times, it's God's whispers telling you to share it.

A few months after my walk on the beach with Jesus, I shared the story with DeeDee. More than two years have passed since then, and I have never felt the need to have that meditation again.

My Mary

I guess I didn't have to, because Jesus had already given me the privilege of walking with Him that day.

Being given such graces comes with a great sense of responsibility. I remember sitting in front of the tabernacle one day and feeling a strong feeling of concern wash over me.

"Father," I prayed, "after all these wonderful graces You have given me, I am afraid. What if I disappoint You?" I started feeling overwhelmed with emotion. "What if I miss what You're telling me You want me to do?"

"Keep doing the work you're doing, Patsy." His voice was clear and gentle in my heart.

When I mentioned my concern to Fr. Ron later, he told me not to put my energy into worrying about disappointing Jesus. Instead, he encouraged me to keep my focus on doing the work I was doing, helping people. It was reassuring to hear these words of support from him. Over these years, I have learned many lessons, but perhaps the most important one is that God will put people in your path when they need to be there for you. This is something for which I am so thankful.

Lenten Mission

(March 2010)

During the first part of the Easter season, the Catholic church usually has a Lenten Mission. This gives the parishioners an opportunity to gather as a community, to be challenged and renewed. I had never attended one. When I read about one that our parish was having, I thought I might like to attend. In my opinion, this mission couldn't have come at a better time for our churches. People were filled with so much anger, hurt, and betrayal because of the sexual abuse scandals with which our Catholic churches were dealing. It was a wonderful opportunity for all of us to channel our focus back onto Jesus. This was a time to begin healing as a community, and to build our churches back up.

To kick off the mission in our parish the Sunday before it started, our Archbishop came to speak at our Mass. He left us with a very tough question.

"What are you doing to help build up your parish?"

This question forced me to take a harder look at myself. Was I doing anything to help build up my own parish, or was I just sitting by, waiting for someone else to do the work? If I were to be honest with myself, I had to admit I wasn't doing enough to help my own parish. We all have a responsibility, because of our baptism, to do God's work. Building up our churches is God's work. That's why I helped facilitate the Women of Grace program in my parish. It wasn't guilt I felt, but in my heart I knew what he said

My Mary

was true. This program for women had helped me grow in my faith, and I wanted to help other women grow in their faith.

The mission was more powerful than I had dreamed it would be. Fr. James, who headed it up, had a charismatic personality and a gift for bringing people closer to Jesus. He made us laugh, and he made us cry. Considering the black cloud that had been hanging over our parishes lately, this gave us an opportunity to see the rainbows. It also gave us the hope and encouragement we needed.

When people haven't experienced these events, it's difficult for them to understand how beautiful they are. Now I could understand how some people became so filled with the Holy Spirit; you could see what was happening in their heart by what was reflected on their faces. I actually felt my whole body fill with the Spirit.

On the last night of the mission, Peter called and apologized, saying he couldn't make it home in time for me to have the car. In the past, this would have offered an easy opportunity for me to avoid going to something. But this mission was different. If I had to walk to the church in order not to miss that last night, I would. Fortunately, I had enough money on me so that I could take a taxi.

I guess the reason I'm sharing this is to help you understand that when Jesus is in your heart, and you allow yourself to be filled with Holy Spirit, you will do things you might not have done in the past, like taking a taxi to the parish. Before this, I would have simply passed on the whole thing.

I could no longer deny that I wasn't the same person I'd been. Sometimes we know in our heart that we've changed, but our head takes a bit longer to catch up. I couldn't help but think that if more people allowed themselves to have a closer relationship with Jesus, what a beautiful world this could be.

Gift of Tongues
(April 16, 2010)

When the day of Pentecost had come, they were all together in one place. And suddenly from heaven there came a sound like the rush of a violent wind, and it filled the entire house where they were sitting. Divided tongues, as of fire, appeared among them, and a tongue rested on each of them. All of them were filled with the Holy Spirit and began to speak in other languages, as the Spirit gave them the ability (Acts 2:1-4).

The Scripture teaches that speaking in tongues is a gift from the Holy Spirit. It allows a person to speak in a foreign language they don't actually know. This was known as a "prayer language," in which the speaker praises God.

In April 2010, I attended my third Weekend of Grace conference for Catholic women along with close to three hundred other women. Something wonderful fills the air when that many women congregate in one room, praising God. After attending such a weekend as this, the women all said their hearts were filled with a longing to do God's work to make the world a better place.

I almost hadn't attended this particular conference, but, as I've said a few times in this book already, when God wants you to be somewhere, things will fall into place to get you there. A couple of months before the conference, I had been speaking to another friend who was also named Rosanne, who I'd barely gotten to see since we longer worked together. By this point I had planned to go to the conference, but I hadn't yet registered. I always looked forward to participating in them. Then Rosanne told me that she and her husband were going on a cruise that month.

"I would love to go on a cruise," I said.

"We're going with a wonderful group," she said. "Why don't you and Peter join us?"

We talked about it some more, and I told her I would discuss it with Peter. They had already booked their places on the cruise months before, so if we wanted to join them we would have to do it as soon as possible. When she told me the week they were going and the date, I realized it was at the same time as the conference.

I felt torn. I wanted to go to the conference, but I also thought it would be nice if we could go on the cruise. Especially since we had never been on a cruise before. That Sunday, when we were at Mass, Peter noticed the brochure for the Weekend of Grace conference in the foyer of our parish.

"Did you know the conference is the same weekend we'd be away?" he asked.

"Yes. I'm really disappointed, but maybe I'm just not meant to attend this year," I replied.

We went to the travel agent and had our trip planned out. Normally, it isn't a problem for Peter to get vacation dates when he puts in for them, and I knew it wouldn't be a problem for me. We told the travel agent we would confirm it the next day, and I sent Rosanne an email saying it was looking great, and we would probably join them on this trip. We were both excited.

But the next day, Peter called me at work and said there was no possible way he could get his vacation at the time that we'd planned to go on the cruise. I was very disappointed at first, but then I started thinking that maybe I was meant to be at the conference after all.

Gift of Tongues

The speaker at this particular conference was very active in the Catholic Charismatic Renewal. She was a gentle women with a faithful presence. This was her second year with us at the conference, and I was glad to see her. It was comforting just hearing her speak. Every speaker at these conferences brings different gifts to help us grow spiritually. I believe her gift was in teaching us how to have the Holy Spirit be more active in our lives. She also spoke about our Blessed Mother, and when she was finished everyone wanted to have a closer relationship the Blessed Mother. She had taught us that by doing so, we would have a closer relationship to her Son.

By the time we got to the end of the second evening, my heart was bursting with happiness and peace. Before the evening ended, we had Adoration, and by this time I was so full of the Holy Spirit I couldn't stay in my seat. I left my friends and went up to sit on the floor in front of the monstrance. A few other people joined me on the floor, including a young girl who was by herself. After a short while, the speaker asked if we would like to be filled with the Holy Spirit. She asked us to take the hand of the person next to us and ask the Holy Spirit to come into our hearts.

I took the young girl's hand, and the next thing I knew, people all around me, including the girl whose hand I held, started to speak in tongues. To my amazement, when I opened my mouth, I was also speaking in tongues. It was almost unbelievable, because it felt so natural for me to speak in this language I didn't even know. It didn't go on for very long, then everything became quiet. The young girl and I looked at one another and smiled.

"I can't believe I just spoke in tongues," I said to her.

She said she had just become a Catholic a couple of weeks before. She had been given the gift of tongues, and had come to the conference hoping she would be able to speak in tongues again. I believe we were both drawn to the monstrance that evening, and I was especially happy to know the person who sat next to me was

My Mary

someone who had recently been given the gift herself. This event was exciting for both of us. We gave each other a hug and went back to our friends.

Last year at the conference, when people started to speak in tongues, I didn't get it. I spoke to my parish priest, Fr. Ron, about it, asking if this was a gift I should want, because I actually felt no real desire to speak in tongues. To be honest, I thought if the Holy Spirit was giving out gifts, I would prefer to receive the gift of wisdom or something similar to that.

I'd grown so much over that one year. What I had learned was that whatever the Father wanted to bestow on me, I would be grateful and say, "Thank You." I also learned and came to believe that He knows best. I knew in my heart why my plans for the trip hadn't worked out: Jesus had known my heart and spirit would be open to receive, and I was ready to receive this gift.

It has been over a year since that conference, and I haven't spoken in tongues since. Maybe someday I will again, but for now I just enjoy the peace that comes from my relationship with Jesus and our Blessed Mother.

Vision of the Blessed Mother

(January 11, 2011)

In the sixth month the angel Gabriel was sent by God to a town in Galilee called Nazareth, to a virgin engaged to a man whose name was Joseph, of the house of David. The virgin's name was Mary. And he came to her and said, "Greetings, favoured one! The Lord is with you." But she was much perplexed by his words and pondered what sort of greeting this might be. The angel said to her, "Do not be afraid, Mary, for you have found favour with God. And now, you will conceive in your womb and bear a son, and you will name him Jesus. He will be great, and will be called the Son of the Most High, and the Lord God will give to him the throne of his ancestor David. He will reign over the house of Jacob for ever, and of his kingdom there will be no end." Mary said to the angel, "How can this be, since I am a virgin?" The angel said to her, "The Holy Spirit will come upon you, and the power of the Most High will overshadow you; therefore the child to be born will be holy; he will be called Son of God. And now, your relative Elizabeth in her old age has also conceived a son; and this is the six month for her who was said to be barren. For nothing will be impossible with God." Then Mary said, "Here am I, the servant of the Lord: let it be with me according to your word." Then the angel departed from her (Luke 1:26-38).

My Mary

There's usually something that sparks a fire in us, that causes us sometimes to do things that we never dreamed possible. For me, it was writing this book after I had a vision of our Blessed Mother.

It's hard to explain, and it's hard to understand as well. About a minute before I opened my eyes that morning in January, I had a vision of the Blessed Mother. Although I had never met DeeDee's aunt, Sister Chris, I believe she is an important part of this story. As I mentioned earlier, Sister Chris was the person who had introduced Adam to our Blessed Mother. She had been the one to give him the little statue which eventually brought him such great comfort when he was coping with his terminal illness.

The week before I had this vision, Sister Chris passed away. On the day DeeDee shared this with us, I was at a Women of Grace program at my parish. I had attended the same program with DeeDee a few years back. We had been participants then. Now we, along with Ella and Marion, were facilitators.

The four of us had been in the first group together, so we felt we knew Sister Chris fairly well because DeeDee always shared stories about her. We also felt that between the four of us we had a special bond, because we wanted very much to help women grow in their faith. Each session, before the other ladies in the group arrived, we four always said a prayer, wanting the women who were attending to develop a closer relationship with Jesus and Mary. At the end of the session, after everyone left, we said another prayer together. We all felt the Holy Spirit was leading our group, and we were so happy to be part of it.

Before I opened my eyes that morning, I saw something beautiful. Before me was a very real, moving vision of our Blessed Mother, standing between two gentlemen wearing black uniforms. I do not remember seeing a white collar, so I didn't get the impression they were priests. Behind her I saw a large, perfect white circle. The two gentlemen stood very still, and though I knew they were

Vision of the Blessed Mother

there, I have no idea what they looked like. I couldn't take my eyes off our Blessed Mother and the perfect bright white circle behind her. She wore a beautiful, full white dress covered in navy prints.

As soon as I opened my eyes, the vision was gone. I felt a strong urge to put my cross necklace on and felt compelled to have it close to me all day. When I got to work that morning, I couldn't keep the experience to myself. I shared what had happened to me that morning with a few of the ladies. I found I could speak more openly about my spiritual experiences by now.

The next evening, I had a meeting at my parish. After the meeting, I spoke to my parish priest, Fr. Ron, about my vision. "What do you think this means?" I asked. "And why was there a large moon behind Mary?"

"How do you know it was a moon?" he asked.

"I don't, but it was a large white perfect circle, so I assumed it was a moon."

He thought about it for a few moments, then asked, "Patsy, what else is white and a perfect circle?"

I frowned. "I'm not sure."

"The Eucharist," he replied. "The two gentlemen you saw could have represented the Son and the Holy Spirit. The circle, the Father, all with our Blessed Mother."

I could understand exactly why he thought this is what it may have represented. I stared at him in shock, in awe that I had been given this grace. Fr. Ron explained to me that sometimes people are given graces when they are trying to bring people closer to our Blessed Mother and Jesus. When I walked away from my parish that evening, I was so thankful for such a wonderful moment of grace that it brought tears to my eyes.

I can't explain how or why, but the next morning when I awoke, I knew I was supposed to start writing this book. I had thought for a long time that someday I might write about the moments of grace I had experienced, but I didn't have any idea of when that might be.

A couple of days later, I was at the Women of Grace course. After the four of us said our prayer together, I shared my experience with the ladies. I also told them I was compelled to write a book about my experiences, after having this vision. None of them seemed shocked. Each one of us was trying to do God's work in our own way. We respected the fact that we were all different from each other, and would be called in whatever way God decided. We agreed that we'd all felt a strong call to arrive on this course exactly when we had.

I believe that on the spiritual journey which we had travelled, we had all come to believe that with God, anything was possible.

At the end of this course, we were all given crosses with different sayings on them. My cross still sits on my windowsill and every time I look at it I'm reminded once again, that nothing is impossible when it comes to God.

But Jesus looked at them and said, "For mortals it is impossible, but for God all things are possible" (Matthew 19:26).

The next Sunday at Mass, I approached one of the ladies who had been in the Women of Grace course with me. Anne is a very spiritual lady who knows a great deal about her faith. I told her about my vision, and mentioned the navy prints that were all over the Blessed Mother's dress. I couldn't remember what the prints were exactly, and that fact was bothering me. I've seen lots of pictures of the Blessed Mother, but she had never been in a dress like the one I'd seen. I kept thinking that this detail was very important.

Anne told me to pray to our Blessed Mother and ask her to show me. I kept thinking about her dress and wondering if maybe the prints weren't important at all. I decided not to worry about it.

Vision of the Blessed Mother

If they were important, I believed she would eventually show me what they were.

A couple of weeks later I was at my physio appointment, waiting for my therapist. When she was ready for me, my therapist came into the waiting room, and I looked up as she walked towards me. I couldn't take my eyes off the white t-shirt she was wearing and my heart began to race. The shirt was covered with navy bows. I could clearly see this was the same print that had been all over Mary's dress. I'd had this same therapist a couple of times before. She is a petite young girl, with long brown hair, and a beautiful, almost innocent face. As she is working with me that night, I couldn't help but wonder if this was what Mary had looked like when she was a young girl.

I still wondered about the navy bows. Since Mary had taken the time to show me what she had been wearing, I assumed this must be an important detail.

A couple of months later, I was having coffee with my friend, Martha, and she asked me how the book was coming along. We started to talk about all the different experiences I'd had, and because she was also a good friend of DeeDee's, this topic was sensitive for her, also. When I told Martha about my physio appointment and the therapist with the navy bows all over her white top, she offered her own take on it. She suggested that the therapist was a healer, so maybe this experience had something to do with healing.

I'll just have to trust that I will know when the Blessed Mother wants me to know.

Our Lady of the Pond

(May 8, 2011)

Sister Chris, Adam's great aunt, had dreamed that a statue of Mary would be placed in the Rosary Garden which Adam's family had so lovingly built in his memory.

As I finished writing that last sentence, I felt a strong urge to go to the Rosary Garden. I'm not usually impulsive, but I grabbed my car keys and told my husband I was going to the Rosary Garden for a little while. He never questions why I need to go there. I think by now he understands that sometimes I just have to trust my intuition on certain impulses.

A strong feeling came over me, and I knew I needed to sit in front of the statue before I wrote about it. It was a beautiful, sunny day, and I sat on the bench so I could look at her. I believe that in order to help me bring people closer to her Son, I need to ask her to help me, and by now I understand that her heart's desire is that we become closer to her Son. I probably sat there for half an hour, enjoying the quiet time with Mary. I know it's not necessary to sit in front of a statue or a picture to pray to her, but what a beautiful gift it was to be able to do this in the Rosary Garden.

DeeDee had kept the statue in the church for a few years. It needed some restoration work, and the timing hadn't yet been right to put it up. Sister Chris had been living in the motherhouse with other Sisters of Charity for many years. When it was time for the building to be torn down, they had many items to distribute to churches or other places who would benefit from their possessions. The statue that was chosen for the garden hadn't been the first one DeeDee had picked out.

Sister Chris asked her which one she had chosen for the Garden, and when she told her, she asked why she hadn't picked the one that was overlooking the pond. That one had obviously been Sister Chris's favourite. Like Sister Chris, DeeDee also felt that this was the most beautiful statue of all the ones that she saw there, but felt maybe it should go to someone else.

Sister Chris insisted that this was the statue that should go in the garden. It had originally been called "Our Lady of the Poor," and it had travelled the world to reach the motherhouse at Mount St. Vincent. It found a home overlooking a pool of water on the convent grounds. For this reason, the Sisters of Charity had fondly called the statue of our Blessed Mother "Our Lady of the Pond."

"Our Lady of the Pond" began its journey in Belgium, where it was purchased by a lady from New York. She donated the statue to be placed on the grounds of the new convent in Halifax, which had been built to replace the old one that had been destroyed in a fire. From 1957 until the day DeeDee took the statue to be put in the Rosary Garden, the Sisters' beloved lady welcomed everyone to the convent from her post by the main entrance.

When DeeDee went to pick up the statue and bring her to the parish until she could be placed permanently in the Garden, she was greeted by one of the sisters. The sister told her they hadn't been expecting her to come for the statue until the following day. She said they had written in their book that she would be picking it up on September 9th. DeeDee had written down that she would be picking it up on September 8th. Since DeeDee was there anyway, they said she could take the statue. Once DeeDee got it to her parish, she had a conversation with Deacon Bernie and explained the mix-up about the dates.

Our Lady of the Pond

"Of course," he said. "It's only right for you to bring Mary home on her birthday."

DeeDee hadn't realized that September 8th was the birthday of our Blessed Mother.

Sister Chris died in early January 2011. Shortly after that, DeeDee started to make plans about having the statue placed in the Rosary Garden, hoping to celebrate Sister Chris's life. After all, it had been Sister Chris who had introduced Adam to the Blessed

Our Blessed Mother statue placed in the Rosary Garden, May 8, 2011

My Mary

Mother. She had attempted to erect the statue a couple of times before this, but always seemed to run into setbacks. After Sister Chris died, and DeeDee decided this time it should go up, everything fell into place.

On Mother's Day, May 8th, 2011, the statue went up.

I couldn't think of a more perfect day for this to take place. We all went to Mass to begin the celebration, then we went out to the Garden. The statue had been covered, and up until the moment of the unveiling I hadn't seen it. The unveiling was exciting, and when the statue was revealed, she was just beautiful. Fr. Chinedu blessed the statue, and we all stood back and admired her. It was a glorious, full circle moment. Our Blessed Mother was now in the Garden where she was meant to be.

There was no doubt in my mind that both Sister Chris and Adam were looking down on us that day, smiling.

After the statue went up, I was told a couple of little stories about the Rosary Garden. One was about a gentleman who spent the night in the garden. I couldn't help but smile, thinking Mary had watched over him all night.

One early morning, Deacon Bernie received a call from the secretary of the parish. The parish priest hadn't been available, so the deacon was called instead. He was told a gentleman had come to the parish office, asking if he could have bus money to get back to where he had previously lived. The deacon arrived at the parish and met the young man, who shared many things about his life that touched the deacon. He immediately felt a bond with the young man.

The man had grown up in Nova Scotia, and in his younger days, he had been a troubled child, causing his family a great deal of stress. Now he was trying to get his life back on track. He had moved out of the province years before, but he had wanted to come back to his roots. After he moved back, he tried making amends with his family, but no matter how hard he tried, his family would not forgive him. They wouldn't let him forget the life choices he had made, the ones of which they were still ashamed.

He knew in his heart he wasn't the same person he'd been years earlier, but he couldn't convince them of that. Although he wanted to stay in Nova Scotia, it became to hard for him to stand the constant rejection from his family.

So he packed all his belongings into a duffel bag and headed to the parish, hoping he could raise enough money for the bus trip back out of Nova Scotia. By the time he got to the parish, no one was around, so he'd gone to the Rosary Garden to spend the night.

After they finished talking, the deacon gave him enough money for a one-way ticket and lunch, then told him he would drive him to the bus stop.

He was visibly grateful. "I just have to go get my bag," he said.

The deacon watched him make his way over to the Rosary Garden and pick up his bag, in which were all his earthly belongings.

"I'm surprised you left that there, unguarded," the deacon said.

"I knew it would be safe."

We never really know how we will impact people's lives. After many months, this young man still keeps in touch with the deacon. He settled back into the place where he had moved after leaving Nova Scotia many years before, and he was doing well. Because of this short crossing of paths, the two men formed a friendship.

On another morning, as the deacon was heading into the parish, he noticed a gentleman dressed in black, kneeling in the Rosary Garden. It was very early, so he was surprised to find anyone there. He'd never seen anyone kneeling like that before, in the outside garden. A short time later, the man approached the deacon. He had just returned to Nova Scotia and was trying to find his way back to the church after having been absent for many years. He attended Mass that morning, then went on his way.

My Mary

These two gentlemen were drawn to the Rosary Garden: one trying to understand forgiveness, the other attempting to find his way back to God. Both were now one step closer to trusting in a higher power.

Beautiful Teaching Moment
(May 14, 2011)

I always looked forward to attending the Weekend of Grace conference. Over the past few years, it had helped me grow spiritually and had introduced me to so many women who also wanted to have a closer relationship to Jesus and Mary. Every year I seem to enjoy it more. The difference this year was that I was asked to take on a little job: being responsible for setting up the communion stations. It would be my responsibility to make sure the line-ups ran smoothly as people came forward to receive the Eucharist and Precious Blood.

The afternoon before we were to have Mass, I went over to the hotel, wanting to make sure I knew beforehand where everyone would be stationed. It was important to me that I did a good job with this task. The morning of the Mass, I spoke to all the ladies involved, then went to speak to Fr. Mark, who was the conference chaplain.

Like when most people get busy, I only had one thing on my mind that morning. I wanted to do the job as well as I could. It's easy to forget the real reason we attend a conference such as this. It's sad, really, how quickly we can forget what Jesus did for us, and take it for granted. In moments like this, it becomes about us and not about Him.

When the bread and wine are consecrated, they are referred to as the Eucharist and Blood of Jesus. When I spoke to Fr. Mark on the morning of the Mass, I was so distracted that I referred to the consecrated Body and Blood as bread and wine. He was very kind, but he told me that I was technically incorrect.

"It is the Eucharist and the Precious Blood," he said.

I hadn't heard a lot of people refer to the consecrated Blood as "Precious." This brought on a whole new meaning for me. It was beautiful to hear him speak of the blood that Jesus shed for us, calling it Precious. It stirred up emotions in me, as if something in my soul had been touched.

When I joined the other ladies, I told them what I had said, and what he had told me. We all occasionally say things that come out incorrectly. I enjoy being made aware of things like this, so I can share them, and others may also learn. As we were leaving the conference that evening, Agnes, one of the ladies called out to me as I was walking away.

"Patsy, that was a teachable moment!"

I smiled at her. "It certainly was," I replied.

The words *Precious Blood* kept coming to my mind after that. One day as Peter and I were driving, I had lots of time to think. My mind went back over what Fr. Mark had said to me that morning, and I wondered why we didn't always refer to Jesus's blood as precious. He certainly deserved it. He shed His blood for us as a free decision of His own, as a holy sacrifice for our sins.

The more I grew spiritually, the more reverence I had towards the Eucharist. I knew that from now on, whenever I received Jesus's Blood in Communion, the word *precious* would always come to mind.

The more I thought about this teaching moment, the more I became convinced that it was no coincidence that it was Fr. Mark who had spoken those words to me. He was the same priest who had journeyed with Adam from the time he'd been diagnosed with cancer until his death. He'd also performed Adam's funeral. When the Rosary Garden was complete, he did the blessing for it.

Beautiful Teaching Moment

Every day I increasingly believe that we have a connection to heaven. I also believe I am supposed to write this book, and I am being guided to do so. I can just picture Adam whispering to Fr. Mark that day, "Correct her when she uses those words. They will touch her heart, and she will remind others that Jesus always wants to be remembered."

> *Who, though he was in the form of God, did not regard equality with God as something to be exploited, but emptied himself, taking the form of a slave, being born in human likeness. And being found in human form, he humbled himself and became obedient to the point of death—even on a cross. Therefore God also highly exalted him and gave him the name that is above every name, so that at the name of Jesus every knee should bend, in heaven and on earth and under the earth, and every tongue should confess that Jesus Christ is Lord, to the glory of God the Father* (Philippians 2:6-11).

We want Jesus to remember us when we are hurting or having difficulties in our lives. It is during those times that we turn to Him the most. If we were to remember Him in our everyday life, we would treat others the way Jesus would treat them, and we wouldn't be so hung up on material things. I remember attending one Mass years ago and will never forget the statement the priest made that day: "You'll never see a U-Haul attached to the back of a hearse."

That statement really stuck with me, because it's so true. We work hard so we can have material things, only to realize we are never satisfied.

I believe Jesus looks down upon us and is sad for our children. A lot of children seem lost today. If we spent more time in prayer with Jesus instead of living as if there were no tomorrow, we would all have more peace in our hearts, and we would make the world a better place for our children. We will not always be with them.

My Mary

When we can no longer help them through difficult times, they will be able to draw from the lessons we taught them. Let us give them the faith that no matter how bad things may get in life, they will never be alone. They can always count on Jesus and our Blessed Mother.

Protection from our Blessed Mother

(May 24, 2011)

There is something about spirituality that makes some people uncomfortable. I'm not the type of person who will push my beliefs on others. What I personally believe is that it is important to try to live a good life, be kind to others, and help whoever God may put in our path. I believe it's not always what you say that may have an impact on people, but how you act.

Once I started being a bit more open about my spiritual journey and sharing it with others, I came to realize that people don't always understand your experiences. So instead of trying to understand that we all have our own journeys, they may make comments to you that make you feel they are making fun of your experiences. We all have different beliefs, and I think it's important for us to try to respect each others' differences.

When I shared with my husband that I felt hurt by some comments that were said to me, he tried to comfort me. "I don't think that person intentionally meant to hurt you," he said. In my heart I knew it was true, but it still hurt. Sometimes we don't realize how much things bother us until someone makes a statement and the hurt comes back to you.

A few days later I was having a conversation with one of my coworkers, Jenny. She mentioned to me that she had been at a focus group the day before. The group had focused on discrimination and on how different religions are discriminated against. To my surprise, the more she talked about it, the more upset I became. The next thing I knew, tears were streaming down my cheeks.

"What's wrong?" she asked, concerned.

I told her I could empathize with the people she'd spoken about. I shared with her some comments that had been said to me, and how much they had hurt my feelings.

"I guess I was more upset than I realized," I admitted.

I don't know about you, but when I'm in the quiet of the night, especially at bedtime, that's when I can sometimes solve my greatest worries and fears. One night I was lying in bed and I started to think about my writing. I recalled the experience that I felt like I was being made fun of. It made me realize that there is a possibility that lots of people could also have this reaction, who didn't understand the things that I experienced. I honestly didn't understand it myself, so I could imagine others may have a hard time with it.

Then I started worrying about people making fun of my family, giving them a hard time. I could just imagine someone saying to my husband or children, "So Jesus has been dropping in on her, has He?"

I'm sure you get the picture. I'd never really given it much thought before that point. I just did what I believed I was supposed to do: share the spiritual journey on which I found myself later in life, share my own experiences with death and healing, and share the lessons I had learned about how we are sometimes called upon to use our experiences to help other people.

Even though I knew that people may make fun of me, I also knew that at the end of the day I would do what I knew in my heart Jesus wanted me to do, no matter what the cost. As I lay in bed that night, I remember wondering who would protect my family. As quickly as the thought came to my mind, so did the answer. I remembered back to when I'd spoken to my priest, Fr. Ron, about my spiritual experiences. I remembered when I was leaving that evening, he'd told me the Blessed Mother would protect me.

I prayed to her that evening, asking for protection. By this time, I'd developed a closer relationship with her, and I knew in my heart she was close by. I knew she'd be with me as I shared my moments of grace, pain, and healing with others.

Memore

Remember, O most gracious Virgin Mary, that never was it known that anyone who fled to your protection, implored your help or sought your intercession, was left unaided. Inspired with this confidence, I fly to you, O Virgin of virgins, my Mother; to you do I come, before you I stand, sinful and sorrowful. O Mother of the Word Incarnate, despise not my petitions, but in your mercy, hear and answer me (Memore from OurLadysWarriors.org).

What a beautiful prayer. It gives hope and comfort, knowing we can go to our Blessed Mother whenever we need her protection or help, or when we need to ask her for help for others. It took a long time for me to develop this relationship with her, but I was so thankful I had it now. She is waiting for each one of us to reach out to her, and when we do, she will somehow let us know that she hears us.

The very next evening after I prayed to our mother for protection, she let me know that she'd heard my prayer to her the night before. I was at an end of the year get together for our Pastoral Ministry at my parish. Fr. Ron was leaving our parish, and I had done a lot of volunteering for our Pastoral Ministry. Just before we sat down to enjoy a meal together, he said he had a picture to give me, to thank me for all the work I'd done over the year.

"It's the picture you love," he said.

My Mary

I knew the one to which he was referring, the beautiful likeness of Jesus holding His mother.

"Thank you," I said, "but I already bought it, as well as a couple of extra copies for people."

As we sat down and began to eat, Fr. Ron presented me with another picture: a large picture of our Blessed Mother. She was absolutely beautiful. Her hands were clasped in prayer, her eyes were looking down. At first glance they almost looked closed. Her gaze reminded me of the vision I'd had of the Blessed Mother. Though she hadn't been dressed the same way, she was looking down at me.

Gifts like this make it impossible for me to doubt that our prayers are heard. There are times we may think they weren't heard, because we don't like the answers we receive. Sometimes we wonder why our prayers aren't being answered, then down the road we are thankful that they weren't. At one time I would have been shocked that this type of thing could happen to me, that I would pray to our Blessed Mother, and she would so profoundly let me know she'd heard me.

As I spent more time in prayer and in learning to trust, I realized that Jesus and Mary are never far away from us. They constantly show us they are close by, but we are so busy with our lives we don't take the time to quiet our minds, and we miss out on these beautiful moments of grace that are right in front us.

Three months after this experience with the picture, I went to a second-hand bookstore to pick out some books for my husband's mother. She loves to read, so every time I visit her I arrive with a stack of books.

When we went to my regular second-hand bookstore, a sign in the window said it had closed down, and it offered an address for another store up the street. When we walked in to the other bookstore, I mentioned to the girl there that I was used to the much

Protection from our Blessed Mother

smaller bookstore down the street. She offered to show me some of the different sections, and I asked her where the spiritual section was.

After I'd picked out the books for Peter's mom, I went back to the spiritual section, though I knew I didn't have a lot of time. We had a four-hour drive ahead of us. I picked up maybe two books, but they just weren't something in which I would be interested. I sent up a quick prayer as I stood in front of the section. "Jesus, if there is something in this section You want me to read, please show it to me."

I know this is difficult to believe, but when I reached for a book to take out of the case, I couldn't help gawking at the cover. It was the exact picture Fr. Ron had given me months earlier, the large, lovely picture of the Blessed Mother. Until I'd received the gift from Fr. Ron, I'd never seen this particular picture of the Blessed Mother. The picture now sits right next to my side of the bed, making me feel as if she is watching over me.

"Oh my God. Peter," I said. "Look at the book I just pulled out."

He recognized the picture Fr. Ron had given me, and knew I wouldn't be leaving that store without it. I was so excited I almost forgot my glasses when I went to pay for it. I just couldn't wait to get in the car and start reading. There's no doubt in my mind that this particular book was picked out for me. The name of the book was *Mother Mary Speaks to Us*, by Brad Steiger and Sherry Hansen Steiger.

I read the back cover and felt incredibly blessed to have come across this book. It made me feel that we just had to open our hearts to Mary, and she would be close to us. Even though we can't always see her she is always with us. Some have been blessed to have had visions of her. I read on the back of the cover of the book, where it said that the purpose of these many sightings is to signal the coming changes. I remembered the vision I had of her myself, and how real it seemed. If this could happen to me, I know it can happen to so many others.

My Mary

She has appeared to many people for many different reasons. I just know that when I had the vision of her, it set me on this journey of actually putting words on paper. It was my turn to share my own spiritual journey. I believe by doing so, others will understand that our Blessed Mother and Jesus want to be a part of our lives.

As I'm writing this section a picture of Jesus pops in my head. It is the picture I have seen many times, and I'm sure you have also. He is knocking on the door and the door knob is only on the inside of the door. He can't go in to be with the person although he wants to, unless that person on the other side of the doors opens it and allows him to enter.

As for my own relationship with the Blessed Mother, I now know this women as a mother. It had taken me many years to establish this relationship with her, but I now understand the love she has for each one of us. She's no longer the beautiful, untouchable queen. She's my mother, and she's your mother, just waiting for us to reach out to her.

As I look up from my computer, the little statue of our Blessed Mother seems to be looking right at me. I hold up the book that I found that day in the bookstore, and though the two faces of Mary are different, I notice that both of them show Mary wearing a white veil, a red dress, and a blue shawl. Mary's hands are folded in prayer in one, while in the other she is pointing to her heart. A thought comes to my mind as I'm looking from one picture to the other.

I can almost imagine her saying, "If you take the time to pray to me, you will touch my heart. In return, I will always keep you close to my Son's heart."

A Numinous Moment

(June 7, 2011)

Numinous: filled with a sense of the presence of divinity; HOLY (Merriam Webster)

Have you ever experienced someone saying something to you, and you assume you must have heard them wrong? You think there is no way on this earth you heard them correctly. I certainly have. I work in a hospital where I am in contact with a lot of women who come in for appointments. My job gives me the opportunity to cross paths with so many people. Considering the short timeframe I have to spend with each person, it's wonderful when a meaningful conversation takes place.

On this particular day, one of the patients approached my work station and asked if I would change her daughter's name in the computer.

"Sure. What is it?" I asked.

"Her name is showing as Pat in the computer," she replied. "I would like it changed to Patricia."

I told her that my name was also Patricia, but I go by Patsy. "It's funny," I mused. "The older I get, the more I feel like a Patricia."

For the past couple of years, I have been feeling like this. It's as if the older we get, the more we become the person we were created to be. I was baptized with the name Patricia. The more spiritual I grow, the more important my baptized name becomes to me. Although it is sometimes hard to face, the reality is that I don't have as many years left to live as the ones I have already lived.

"What's your daughter's middle name?"

"Ann Mary," she replied. "Patricia Ann Mary, and she was born on the Feast of the Holy Rosary."

I stare at the lady in disbelief. "When did you say her birthdate was?"

"October 7th," she replied.

"I can't believe this," I say, my eyes drawn to the cross she is wearing. "I'm writing a book, and the names and birthdate that you just mentioned are a significant part of my book."

The night before, I had received a call from Roseann. She apologized for calling so late, but I told her the timing was great, because I had just finished writing about my mom. Reliving my loved ones' deaths is still very painful for me. I always need a box of Kleenex close by. The night before that, I had written about my Nan.

My name is Patricia. My mom's name is Ann, and my Nan's name is Mary. Adam's birthday was October 7th, the Feast of the Holy Rosary.

I tell the woman this, and we both understand that our meeting that day was meant to be. I felt a spiritual connection with her. Of all the experiences I'd had up to this point in my spiritual journey, this was the one that really blew my mind. Any doubts I'd experienced since the first day I'd sat to write this book were gone.

Sure, I'd had doubts. I questioned why an ordinary person, who is not a writer, would be called to share their journey in book form. I questioned whether my writing was indeed being divinely guided. For someone who is not a writer, I am constantly amazed by how easily the words flow out of my heart. I had never before considered writing a book.

A Numinous Moment

But once I allowed Jesus to take over the wheel, my life changed, and so did I. I understand now, more than ever, how we are all connected. This book is part of my journey. I trust with all my heart that this is exactly what Jesus is calling me to do. I trust with all my heart that I will share my journey exactly the way he wants me to.

Life Lessons

(September 2011)

We learn many life lessons throughout our lives. These lessons come in different forms, and often we learn the hard way. We may even end up with regrets.

I've had my share of life lessons, just like everyone else. Some lessons teach me, and others I may have to experience again until I get it right. When I share this recent life lesson, I feel as if I was in a scene in a movie, almost like it was set up for me. While it was happening it seemed surreal. Then again, considering all the different experiences I've been having, nothing should surprise me anymore.

I had just finished a very busy morning at work. As I went to get my lunch from the staff room, I looked out the window. It was a beautiful September day, and it looked very peaceful outside. The flowers looked beautiful, and park benches were full of people enjoying the sun. I decided I would enjoy my lunch out there. As I looked around for a place to sit, I noticed a gentleman sitting on a bench with his head in his hands. I walked towards the bench from behind him, and he lifted his head. Tears were pouring down his face. He wiped away his tears with a Kleenex, and my heart went out to him.

I'm not the same person I was years ago. Then, I would have looked at this gentleman and probably had the same reaction, but would never have approached him to offer comfort. If I see someone hurting now, I no longer hesitate to offer a word of comfort, or to just listen.

I sat behind him on another bench, but I watched to make sure he was okay. After a few minutes, he still seemed very upset, so I got up and approached him. As he looked up, I smiled and asked if there was anything I could do to help him feel better.

"No, I'm okay," he whispered.

I kept walking and decided to sit on another bench. I was in front of the gentleman, but from where I sit I could see his profile. I gazed towards the road and noticed a man walking directly towards me. He passed other people and stopped right in front of where I was sitting.

"Excuse me," he asked. "Would you have any spare change?"

I glanced at the man, studying him from head to toe. He didn't look like a street person. Actually he was dressed well, and would probably blend in with any crowd. I make a quick decision.

"Sorry. I don't have any spare change," I said, even though I did.

He turned from me and I just knew he would go over to the gentleman who had been crying earlier. As he headed towards him, I distinctly thought the sad man would give this man the money I'd refused to give him. Sure enough, the gentleman reached into his pocket and handed him the money. I immediately felt as if I'd just failed a test that had been given to me. With the money now in his hand, the man walked away and went back to the sidewalk.

I had just been shown a great lesson. Even though I was disappointed in myself, I quickly realized how this would help me in the future, showing me not to judge who God sent into my life for help. It was easy to see that the man with the tears was upset and needed comfort. Maybe not from me, but from someone. But what about the man who'd asked for money? I'd made a judgment and refused to help him.

Life Lessons

Of course, I immediately tried to make myself feel better by justifying my actions. I recalled a time when a street person had ripped me off. I had given that person money. The next day, on my way to work, the lady selling tickets in the lotto booth said she'd seen me giving the man money the day before. "He bought lotto tickets with the money you gave him," she told me.

Sometimes I gave money to street people after that, and other times I didn't. The bottom line, though, is that I so quickly judged the person to whom I would or wouldn't give my money. I looked back at the gentleman who had been upset earlier and marvelled. *My God*, I thought, *you are in so much pain yourself, but you still reached out to help another without hesitation.* What a beautiful thing to witness. I got up from my bench to go back inside, feeling like I'd just had one of those surreal moments in my life.

As I walked by, the gentleman called out to me. "Thank you for offering to help me," he said, smiling.

I smiled back at him. "You're so welcome," I replied, then added, "God bless you."

I couldn't help but think of all the times Jesus sent people to us for help. Many times I'm sure we miss out on the opportunity to help them, because for one reason or another we don't feel it's our responsibility. I guess we need to trust more that Jesus knows each one of our hearts, and what we need. This would be one of those lessons that stayed with me. When Jesus sent people to me for help, I would have to try to judge them not by the way we look at things in the secular world, but rather how Jesus would have treated them.

Before I went back to work, I stopped to talk to one of my coworkers. "Linda, I just had the strangest experience," I said.

I told her what had happened, and how I couldn't help but feel like I was being taught a very important lesson about not judging others. "Do you think I may be right, that this could be possible?"

"Yes, Patsy, I think you may be right," she said.

Linda is a very open-minded person. When these types of things happen to people, it doesn't usually surprise her. She understands that sometimes there's so much more going on in life than what our minds comprehend at that time. After we'd been back at work for a while, I went to share something else with her.

"Linda, I think I know why this happened to me today," I said.

"Why?"

"It's for me to remind people in my book how important it is not to judge others like I did, before we even know what their story may be." I said, and noticed she was smiling at me.

Shortly after this experience, I come across a Bible quote. It reinforced to me what I'd learned in this lesson. Jesus was the teacher, and we were the disciples. We were to learn from Him how to treat our brothers and sisters. Our time on earth should be spent learning how to become more like Him. We might make mistakes along the way, but recognizing those mistakes is how we will become more like Him.

A disciple is not above the teacher, but everyone who is fully qualified will be like the teacher (Luke 6:40).

Come, See, Go, Tell

But the angel said to the women, "Do not be afraid; I know that you are looking for Jesus who was crucified. He is not here; for he has been raised, as he said. Come, see the place where he lay. Then go quickly and tell his disciples, 'He has been raised from the dead, and indeed he is going ahead of you to Galilee; there you will see him.' This is my message for you" (Matthew 28:5-7).

I started to write this book in February. It wasn't any surprise to me that in May, at our Weekend of Grace conference, the theme was "Come, See, Go, Tell." I actually smiled when I saw it, because I was one step ahead.

None of us knows where our life will lead us. Our journey is so personal, and so many people come in and out of our lives. Sometimes it's not until much later that we realize the impact they had on how we would choose our journey. For me, looking back, I understand why I had to go through things that were very painful. I can even understand why sometimes we need to bury our pain. It's so we will be able to survive.

I'm thankful that pain will eventually resurface so that we will be given an opportunity to deal with it, even if it takes years. It helped me become who I am today.

My Mary

I wanted to share my spiritual journey because, in my heart, I honestly believe that is what Jesus and our Blessed Mother want me to do. When we grow through different experiences, we become who we are meant to be. Most times it takes many years to realize this is happening, but time isn't important. What is important is that we use what we learn, and share it, so it may help others who may be struggling on their own journeys.

Spiritually, it took many years for me to get where I am today, and I still have much more to learn. The most important thing I learned through all my experiences was to trust God. He knows what we need, and He will guide us if we let Him.

I am thankful that I learned to quiet my mind so I could hear His whispers and allow Him to guide me.

I am also thankful for all the people that He put in my path. Some of them helped me become who I am today, though they might not have known it. Sometimes we take our families for granted, but we can be sure we were put in those families because these were the people God chose to help us with our spiritual growth.

I came across a short poem years ago that touched my heart. I hope I can look back at the end of my life and be happy, knowing I have accomplished what it says.

> *If I can throw a single ray of light across the darkened pathway of another,*
> *If I can aid some soul to clearer sight of life and duty, and thus bless my brother,*
> *If I can wipe from any human cheek a tear, I shall not have lived my life in vain while here.*
> Author Anonymous
> *The Power of Prayer* (Publications International Ltd. 1998)

Come, See, Go, Tell

Isn't it wonderful that we are given a new slate every day? We are given, by the grace of God, free will to do whatever we want with our lives. We can turn our back on Him, or we can spend time with Him, becoming more like Him. My hope for you, all my brothers and sisters, is that you allow yourself to experience all the precious moments of grace that the Father so happily gives each one of His children.

The title of this book was not the original one I had planned. I started with *Moments of Grace,* because that was exactly what I had been given. Then I was gently corrected about the Eucharist and Precious Blood, and I kept thinking I should somehow include Jesus's Precious Blood in the title.

When I mentioned I was struggling with a title, I was told by a few people not to even think about it. They said the title would come to me when it was supposed to, so I tried to push my concern over choosing a title to the back of my mind until I was finished writing. One day I was out walking, and I began to ponder the title again. Even though I had been trying to put it out of my mind, I guess the timing was right.

I considered both of the titles I had chosen.

Yes, I had been given beautiful moments of grace.

Yes, I desperately wanted people to look at Jesus's Blood as precious, since I could no longer see it any other way.

But in the end, it was our Blessed Mother who I couldn't get out of my mind. I now understood that through the Blessed Mother we can have a closer relationship to her Son, Jesus. Through Jesus, we can have a closer relationship to His Father.

My mind kept going back to the little statue that had once been given to a three-year-old boy. I thought about how important this statue had become in comforting a young man facing his death. I considered the impact Sister Chris had made on so many lives by giving this little statue as a gift. When I learned of the

My Mary

depths of a little boy's love of the Blessed Mother, that helped me reach out to her as my own mother.

Many people visit the Rosary Garden that was built in memory of Adam. I thought back to the story of little Adam putting his arms around the big statue of Mary and calling out "My Mary!" We can all learn so much from this little boy.

The Blessed Mother is our Mary. She is there for all us. If you wish to have a closer relationship to her Son, reach out to her.

My Mary. I knew as soon as the words were out of my mouth that it was the perfect title for this book. As I finished my walk, my heart was full of joy, knowing that the title had indeed come to me. Just as quickly, a thought came to my mind. Was I the one who had actually picked out the title? I smiled. Probably not. Not only was Adam up there in heaven now, but Sister Chris as well. There was no doubt in my mind that one of them had whispered the title to me.

With all the different things I had experienced since the night Adam died, it is no surprise to me that later that evening I was given a sign confirming that *My Mary* was the perfect title. As I was running my bath, I reached for a bar of soap and realized we had none left. I went into the kitchen and asked Peter if he knew if there were any extra bars around.

"Look in my shaving bag," he says.

I keep a basket in the bathroom, which holds different bath products. I was pleased to see a little bar of soap sitting on the top of the basket. The soap was in the shape of an angel, still in its plastic. I picked it up and examined it as I headed back down the hall to tell Peter I'd found soap. I suddenly realized where this bar of soap had come from. It had been part of a Christmas gift from Adam's mom, DeeDee.

I couldn't help but laugh and send up a little message. "Thanks for the sign. *My Mary* it is."

Will You Carry My Son in Your Heart?

We know that at the moment of the Annunciation, the Blessed Virgin Mary was uniquely commissioned to bring Jesus into the world. She was to become the perfect channel of God's greatest Gift. That is why we esteem her above all the saints. God entrusted this singular and holy honour to Mary alone, but in a certain sense, God extended the call He'd issued to Mary to each of us, asking Will you bring my Son into the world?

Will you carry Him in the womb of your heart as Mary carried Him in the womb of her body? Will you birth Him into the lives of others, that all might come to experience the grace of redemption and eternal life?

Like the Blessed Mother, you and I have a choice. We can say "yes" to God's request, or we can say "no." And, just like Mary's response, our answer has eternal consequences, both in our lives and in the lives of others. If we say "yes," as Mary did, God will empower us with His Holy Spirit. We, too, will be filled with the life of Jesus Christ. Like Mary, we will become a channel of grace through which the love of God enters the world. And because the spiritual needs of our day are so great, all of heaven is holding its breath, waiting for our response.

(Full of Grace, Johnnette S. Benkovic)

My Mary

How comforting to know that if we say yes, we will also be empowered with the Holy Spirit to do God's work. I remember the day DeeDee brought a small book called *Mary, Did You Know* to my house. It had a CD inside. As I listened to the words on the CD, I couldn't help but wonder about the day that Mary had said "yes" to God. She probably didn't realize at that time the impact that her answer would have on the world. We also don't know the impact that our "yes" to God will have on the world.

Our "yes" will help to make the world a place where love is in the forefront. A place where we are willing to be there for each other, in good times and in bad. A world that is not ruled by how much we can acquire, but by how much we can help our brother and sister in time of need. A world where people know in their heart the love and mercy that our Father has for each one of us, and no matter what life may bring us we will never be alone. Such a big question to be asked. What will our answer be?

I can only share with you my own experience when I said "yes" to God. Every one of our own spiritual journeys will be different, but God will be at the centre. He'll be there to walk beside us so that no matter how bad things may get in our life, we can always have faith and hope that we will get through it with His grace.

Because of my own "yes," I have been blessed to be given many opportunities that have helped me grow in my Catholic faith. Once my heart became filled with the Holy Spirit, I don't think anything could have stopped me from learning everything I could that would help me do what I believed was being asked of me. To help comfort God's people. Once I slowed down enough to hear those whispers clearer, I ran with it like wild fire.

The past four years of this journey has taken me in so many different directions. All along the way so many spiritual people were put in my path. People who I could learn from and people who could learn from my experiences.

I found myself working with children and adults in the bereavement field, journeying with the dying, visiting the sick, taking a Women of Grace program, and then helping to facilitate the program in my own parish. I also attended many conferences for Catholic women. Not just to grow in my faith but to experience being together with so many women in one place who also wanted to make the world a better place. A place where God would be at the centre of all our decisions.

I'm hearing those whispers again. I believe He is letting me know that this part of the journey is completed. I did the work that He had wanted me to learn, and now He has another plan for me. I do not know what this plan will be, but I do know that I can trust that He will lead me. I believe it's important for me to share my story with others.

God has plans for every one of us. He just asks that we take some time to spend with Him with an open heart, to hear those whispers. If God whispered something in your ear, would you slow down long enough to hear what He is saying?

References

Benkovic, Johnnette, *Full of Grace: Women and the Abundant Life*, copyright © 2004. Used with permission.

Catechism of the Catholic Church, second edition, copyright © Concacan Inc.—Libreria Editrice Vaticana, 1994, 1997, for the English translation in Canada. All rights reserved. Used with permission.

Diary, Saint Maria Faustina Kowalska, *Divine Mercy in My Soul* copyright © 1987 Congregation of the Marians of the Immaculate Conception of the B.V.M, Stockbridge, MA 01263. Used with permission.

Heald, Cynthia, "The Father and the Child." *Drawing Near to the Heart of God,* Colorado Springs, CO: NavPress (www.navpress.com). All rights reserved. Used with permission.

Holy Bible, NRSV Catholic Edition, Harper Collins Publishers, 1989.

Merriam Webster

OurLadysWarriors.org, "Memore." Used with permission.

Smith, Carol, "Angels are Watching." *Angels: Heavenly Blessings*. Publications International, 1998. Used with permission.

My Mary

Wilde, Gary, *The Power of Prayer*, Publications International Ltd. 1998. Used with permission.

www.ingramcontent.com/pod-product-compliance
Lightning Source LLC
Chambersburg PA
CBHW060514090426
42735CB00011B/2221